Feminine Wiles
Creative Techniques for Writing Women's Feature Stories that Sell

by
Donna Elizabeth Boetig

Clovis, California

Quill Driver Books/Word Dancer Press, Inc.
8386 N. Madsen Avenue
Clovis, California 93611

Printed in the United States of America
Second Printing April 1999

Quill Driver Books/Word Dancer Press books may be purchased at special
prices for educational, fund-raising, business or promotional use.
Please contact:

Special Markets
Quill Driver Books/Word Dancer Press, Inc.
8386 N. Madsen Avenue
Clovis, California 93611
800-497-4909

To order another copy of this book please call
800-497-4909

ISBN 1-884956-02-5

Quill Driver Books/Word Dancer Press
Project Cadre
Stephen Blake Mettee
Marilyn Harper McDaniel
Cindy Wathen
Linda Kay Weber

Boetig, Donna Elizabeth, 1950 —
    Feminine wiles : creative techniques for writing women's feature
stories that sell / by Donna Elizabeth Boetig.
        p.   cm.
    ISBN (invalid) 1-884956-02-5 (pbk. : alk. paper)
    1. Feature writing.   2. Womens periodicals.   I. Title.
PN4784.F37B64   1998
808'.02--DC21   98-13793
                                                                    CIP

❦ Contents

The Bye Lines

Acknowledgments

I would like to thank the editors who taught me to write on the job especially Melody Dahl of *The Hampton Union,* New Hampshire, Andrew Ratner of *The Baltimore Sun,* Stephanie Abarbanel of *Woman's Day* and Susan France of *Reader's Digest.*

Also appreciation to David Everett, coordinator of the Washington, D.C. graduate writing program of Johns Hopkins University, for his flexibility and support.

Thanks, too, to writing friend, Linda M. Gosman of Severna Park, Maryland, whose incredible right brain came up with the idea for this book and even titled it one morning over warm pumpkin muffins at Garry's Grill.

I would also like to express my appreciation to Nancy Osius Zimmerman, formerly of St. John's College, Annapolis, Maryland, and Thomas Hunter of Effective Communications Group, Ridgewood, New Jersey, both great writers, friends and cheerleaders extraordinaire. Everyone should know such believers.

My gratitude to my parents, John and Ethel Byrnes of Fairfield, Connecticut, my mother-in-law Constance Boetig of Fountain Hills, Arizona, my husband Allen and our sons, Scott, Bradley and Ryan cannot be put into words. Maybe Ryan expressed it best when, as a toddler, he turned to my mother and said, "My heart is filled with love for you." Ditto to all of the above.

First Musings

M Y FIRST JOURNEY INTO THE FEMININE WILES of writing women's stories began in high school when I wrote about
two girls who were nearly raped at a rural Connecticut lake. The paper
earned an *A* and my teacher's praise. This was my first inkling of the
pleasure that writing women's stories brings.

Still, those years were void of any great intellectual awakenings. To
prove it, at graduation I was awarded two class superlatives: Most Feminine and Biggest Flirt. I studied journalism in college, but instead of entering the newsroom after graduation, I married my college sweetheart Allen.

We settled in Miami, where he commanded a 95-foot patrol boat
and I a classroom of kids: 46 third and fourth graders who had just come
to the mainland from Cuba—this was 1972. They spoke only Spanish and
I spoke only English. No wonder I thought it would be easier to get pregnant and take care of only one child.

Our sons, Scott and Bradley, were born 19 months apart. I loved
domesticity. I also loved not going back to those 46 kids. One afternoon,
while the babies napped, I leafed through an old copy of *Writer's Market*.
There was something enticing about the alphabetized listings of hundreds
of publications all seeking writers to develop ideas, interview, write, publish. But then the babies awoke, and it was time to read books and walk in
the woods with the dogs, identifying birds, naming trees. Back home, I
had a lot to learn too: stenciling, gourmet cooking, antiquing. My urge to
write was suppressed by creative outlets within the walls of home.

When our family moved to New Hampshire, my new neighbor Phyllis
and I became quick friends. This quick-witted, Irish mother of three who
was in the throes of a divorce, couldn't believe I wasn't "using my college
degree." In the past I refused to let my mother-in-law get away with such
nonsense. I knew better. We use everything we learn, every moment—
especially mothers, I'd counter defensively. But Phyllis was a friend so she
could say such things. Phyllis also encouraged me to apply for a part-time
writing job for our small town paper. I got the job.

One night a week, while Allen cared for the kids, I covered town and
school meetings until midnight, then pulled an all-nighter writing stories.

(I was 29.) The next morning, with Ryan in a backpack—yes, we had a third son—I delivered the copy to the news editor. As I looked over her shoulder she edited the piece, explaining her every move. "Ahhh, this is *great*," she'd enthuse, "but it's too far down the page, move it up." As fate would have it, my "beat" turned hot—protesters fought the licensing of the controversial Seabrook nuclear power plant; four Catholic nuns sued their bishop for breach of their teaching contracts and wound up on the "Today Show" and the local fireworks factory exploded. Writing gave me a paycheck, $65 a week. But more important, writing gave me an identity, apart from being Allen's wife and Scott, Brad and Ryan's mother, I was the town reporter. From there, I wrote for a daily paper in Portsmouth, New Hampshire, and later for the conservative Manchester *Union Leader*.

As our babies grew into boys and we moved to Maryland, writing became an even bigger part of my day. I did a stint as a staff writer from Annapolis for *The Baltimore Sun*, contributing three features a week on education, state politics or lifestyle issues. One day as I sat in city hall covering Youth in Government Day, I figured there had to be a magazine connected with the sponsoring group. I tweaked the article I had written for the *Sun* and submitted it to *The Optimist* magazine. The editor bought it and I was hooked. The exhilaration of creating stories for national publication was addictive. Soon I was writing for the religious magazines, next the brides' magazines, then *Family Circle, Woman's Day, McCall's* and *Reader's Digest*.

Although I began as a generalist following any intriguing story idea— once I wrote a column for *The Saturday Evening Post* about dentists becoming entrepreneurs—eventually I succumbed to the lure of telling women's stories.

These women's tales took me inside worlds I never would have known, including a maximum security prison where mothers with babies at their breasts served life sentences for violent crimes, the scorching Arizona desert where a young woman and her dog found a lost toddler near death and the top of the Utah peaks, where search and rescue volunteers rappel off the mountains with dogs strapped to their backs.

Even more gratifying, these stories introduced me to ordinary women doing extraordinary things. Women like Penny Thomas who risked her own child's life to save another and Sandy Barnes who—in the depth of despair over her little boy's death—donated his liver to a young woman named Maria. Maria named her first born after Sandy's son, then asked Sandy to be his godmother. And the story of Grace Corrigan, the mother of teacher-in-space Christa McAuliffe, who, a decade after her daughter's death in the Challenger space shuttle explosion, leads a life of courage.

Some of the stories I wrote for women's magazines weren't about women at all, like the drama of Gary Chenoweth, a single dad devoted to nurturing his two desperately ill sons.

About 10 years ago I discovered that the next best thing to writing is teaching writing, sharing with like-minds the obsession of spilling words onto paper. I also experienced the sheer indulgence of earning a graduate writing degree.

Taking and teaching classes gave me an excuse to keep up with my kids, who grew smarter by the day. If I was taking a class, I had to push aside the "I shoulds"—the, I should be doing this, I should be doing that—and let the dishes mount and the dust bunnies pirouette, while I read and wrote. The same was true if I were teaching a class—I couldn't face students unprepared, could I?

Writing also taught me to read, appreciatively. No longer did I whip through pages Evelyn Wood style. Speed reading suddenly seemed as sinful as swallowing shrimp in one gulp. Instead, writing taught me to savor the wonder of words as they rise from the page into my mind—even if these words are from the local paper, a day away from the trash.

And not to be overlooked, writing gave me friends. Some of my closest friends are writers, some are former students. There's a bond among writers that helps friendships deepen faster, maybe it's all that shared anguish *and* exhilaration.

In a phrase, writing's given me a life. And this is no small gift for a boomer mother whose kids are forging their own: Scott's a computer systems consultant based in Philadelphia, Brad's in medical school in Maryland and Ryan's en route to the U.S. Naval Academy.

But I have a future too. I have stories to tell. And I suspect you do too.

❦ ❦ ❦

Feminine Wiles was born over coffee and pumpkin muffins one morning when my writer friend, Lynn, said, "You should write a book about writing women's stories. There's nothing out there like it."

Feminine Wiles is a sharing of truths that I wish I had known when I first began writing women's stories. Some of the lessons are from my own life, others come from editors, teachers, other writers and friends—all of whom I can never thank enough. Consider these strategies, suggestions, secrets—these feminine wiles—as opportunities, never imperatives.

The principles in *Feminine Wiles* have inspired hundreds of my students to write and publish stories that change readers' lives—and their own, too. This is my heartfelt wish for you.

The Chase

At the Starting Line

YOU SHOULD BE PUBLISHED. Your aunt, your best friend, and your third grade teacher with the hairy mole on her left cheek all said the same thing: They liked your writing. You should share your stories with others.

Still, the time has never seemed right. First your husband (or wife) needed you. Then it was the kids. Finally, as you took pen in hand, the dog decided to host a party of Sam's Club-sized fleas. As if these were not enough distractions, there was always the perennial diet. You couldn't write until you lost those extra 10 pounds. After all, you wanted to look svelte in all those press shots.

Lately, though, all the reasons not to write have paled in comparison to the reason to write: You want to do it more than anything in the world. Could it be if you don't, you may *not* live to regret it? You've been daydreaming about your byline in glossy magazines and big city newspapers read by sophisticated people with lattes in one hand and your words in the other. You've envisioned your life as a freelance writer: meeting fascinating people, telling fascinating tales, being fascinating. Now, if the worse fallout from all these visions was a mounting pile of dirty dishes, there would be no problem. But when, cloaked in thoughts of bylines, you cut off an 18-wheeler cruising down a highway at 85, you know the time has come. If you don't write, you may be roadkill.

So commit yourself. You are going to write stories of women's struggles and joys. You are going to discover information that changes the lives of readers. You are going to predict trends and you may even create a few of your own. You are going to look out into the world to see what's happening and take what you find deep within yourself to figure out what it all means—for you, and your readers.

You are going to write about the famous and the ordinary, and you are going to write about yourself.

You are going to learn to draft, write and rewrite a myriad of stories: true life dramas, those of others or your very own; how-to articles that teach the reader anything from how to choose the correct type of lettuce for her next salad to how to travel the world for free; self-help pieces that seem to forever focus on getting thinner, smarter, richer or smugger; roundups that combine three or more mini-stories all melding to make a point. And you are going to write the personal essay in which you open a vein and explore a piece of your self. Your articles will be limited only by the requirement that they provide a rewarding experience for the reader.

Then you are going to find editors at newspapers and magazines, large and small, who will publish your stories.

I am going to walk you through it. I am going to tell you everything I know about writing women's stories. And everything I know about getting them rejected—and even better—getting them published.

By the end of this book, you'll be a better writer. You might even be a better spouse, lover, friend because you'll be doing what you must do. And that's what really matters.

What's the price for all this joy? Commitment. Once you begin, there's no turning back. Not even when the journey gets bumpy, detours and delivers you a migraine. Not even when you eat every potato chip in the house, then drive to the store for more. No excuses. You are not allowed to stop writing to examine your dog for flea infestation, or phone your mother-in-law cross-country, begging her to visit. And you are definitely not allowed to long for those before publication days, those days when you wiled away hours reading junk, watching CNN or contemplating the shadows moving across your patio, all without a twinge of the "I shoulds." The I should be reading something good. I should be writing.

Now, if you are a male reading this, I am sure there are equally uncomfortable situations you can conjure up. Let your mind run wild. And, by the way, welcome. Lots of men write women's stories. It's a wide-open, lucrative market. For years *Family Circle* magazine ran an extremely popular back page essay written by a man. *Glamour* still features "Jake: A Man's Opinion." Bridal magazines are always hyping stories about what *really* goes on at those bachelor parties. *Redbook* writes about what turns men on, and one major women's magazine (sorry my perimenopausal mind can't recall which) featured an article on how to decorate a bedroom for romance—written by a man. Editors are hungry for the male point of view. Indeed, your other-sex status may serve you well.

Once you have felt the first pulse of publication, once you've realized the dream is only as far away as your fingertips, your life will never be the same. It's like becoming a parent or even becoming real like the Velveteen Rabbit. You'll lose some things, but you'll gain far more. Grab a pad and a pen, and let's begin.

Faces of Eve

TELL SOMEONE YOU'RE WRITING WOMEN'S STORIES and you'll be met with one of two reactions. Either she'll start reciting a few lines from Deborah Tannen's tome on the differences in communication between the sexes, *You Just Don't Understand,* or she'll bristle, "There's no difference, good writing is good writing."

Hmmm.

Anyone who believes men and women approach stories with like-attitudes has only to eavesdrop on my husband Allen and me. Trying to forge a bond between the hours he spends in Washington D.C. negotiating ship building contracts with the government and my days in suburban Maryland negotiating words with editors, I beg for connection. I corner him on the sofa or across the kitchen table as soon as he gets home. My body close to his.

I barrage him with questions, Socrates-style. When one strikes a spark, I fan the flame. "Now how did he say it?" I may ask. "What were his exact words?" I beg for details, I pry for the sensation that led up to the moment he's deigned to discuss—even if the topic's as tepid as an addendum to a contract. My husband looks at me as if I should be trying out for a role in *One Flew Over the Cuckoo's Nest.*

Allen wants facts. I want intimacy. Allen converses to get information. I tell stories and listen to show I care. I like beginnings, middles and ends. He likes conclusions: "What's the point?" I like to tease, to seduce my husband, to bring him in with an enticing tidbit, then hold his attention with a morsel at a time. He wants none of this. He wants the entrée.

"So what happened?" he asks anxiously. "Did she get the job or not?"

To him, the rest is yadda, yadda, yadda. And if any of these meanderings take on a metaphysical or philosophical bent, especially if he's got tennis on the brain, I might as well talk to our Lab, Chester. Now this is not to say that Allen's never in the mood for a "soul out" as he calls them, but the time and place has got to be right. Not so with me. To me, this verbal intercourse is about connection. It's the Hall-mark card without the stamp. The one I like to give and like better to receive.

I know not all men are like Allen. There are those who linger lov-ingly over each sigh. (On the other hand, I've also known women who lunge for the jugular in conversations.) My father, for one—after 52 years of being married to my mother—still relishes listening to every nuance as she recalls her women's luncheon conversations. My friend, Kathy, and her husband, Dave, also share such verbal intimacy—one that I, ironically, find a bit *too* cozy. I've been taken aback more than once by Dave's comments on something I intended only for his wife's ears, unaware he is to be included in our conversational loop.

To Allen and many men, one of the benefits of a long loving rela-tionship is the absence of speaking the obvious. It's the privilege of en-joying a silence that needs no words. It's the joy of knowing your part-ner silently fills in the lashes on the portrait of your relationship.

I'm not saying one sex's approach to communications is superior to the other, it's just different. And knowing this and embracing it helps a whole lot when we write stories. Now you'd think men would have a tougher time making this leap to feminine communication. Not so. Maybe it's because men suspect they might have to approach women readers a little differently than they would their own sex, that they do just that—and many succeed to a far greater degree than some women writers. Women, on the other hand, can become complacent when writ-ing to other women, assuming it's second nature to converse with our sisters. Not necessarily. Any writer, of either sex, can touch the reader profoundly, if he or she cares enough to capitalize on what makes a woman's story different.

Let's start with the main course of any talk about sexual differ-ences: emotion. Men and women share many of the same basic feel-ings—but not to the same intensity, researchers say. Besides, women's emotions are often related to internal sources, such as guilt or anxiety, while men's revolve around external triggers such as physical action or an angry confrontation. Recurrently, when women sit down to talk, the experiences they choose to focus on are emotional—often relation-ships entangled with sadness or fear.

It's no surprise that women, more than their testosterone bearing counterparts, reveal feelings through facial expressions and gestures.

Why am I telling you all this? Same reason that you learned where the Mississippi River is, although you may never cross it. It's necessary background. This is the stuff that seeps into your subconscious and somehow makes you a better writer of women's stories.

Let's see how you can weave this into your work. Since women communicate their feelings through facial expressions and body gestures, skim a book on body language, picking up concepts and ideas. But don't interpret in your stories or articles what a woman's motions mean, just note them. Your subject grimaces or grins. She blinks quickly or bites her lip. Your reader will take it from there.

Remember how reporters captured Christa McAuliffe's emotion when she was selected by Vice President Bush to become the first teacher in space? Flanked by squeaky-clean NASA types and the other teachers she bested for the shuttle seat, she walked to the center of the stage and proclaimed into the microphone, "When that shuttle goes up, there may be only one teacher aboard..." then—and here's the part every reporter noted—Christa took her index and middle fingers and pressed them to her lips, paused a few seconds and then finished, "but I'll be taking ten souls with me." The reporters didn't explain that Christa's voice cracked or her eyes welled up. They didn't need to. They provided the one telling detail that communicates this to the reader. Readers figured it out and were grateful.

Suppose your subject was tapped for promotion but knew all along the new job was hers. How did her intuition speak in the physical? Reporting her ever so subtle expression or gesture will be more gratifying to your reader than if you just come out and say she felt the job was hers all along.

Women, being intuitive, are quick to interpret the expressions and gestures of others. If you want to nail down when the wife of a cheating husband first sensed something was awry in their storybook marriage, ask her for the revealing details: his expressions, his glances everywhere but in her direction, his speech contradictions, hesitations or repetitions.

From birth, men tend to place physical evidence above insight. They're literal creatures, so when we write stories they read we'll go lightly on the allusions or nuances. They require proof, tangible evidence. Not so with women who are convinced by a feeling or even a fleeting sensation.

Feminine readers will pick up the meaning behind these silent messages and thank you for not spelling it out.

Realize, too, that when a woman's telling you her story, she's often coloring it with the magic marker of me-blame. As women, we tend to believe that when something goes wrong, anything, somehow the finger of blame points to us.

This reminds me of a comment my friend, Sue Campbell, an editor for the *St. Paul Pioneer Press* in Minnesota made about the stories she chooses for her life-styles section. "My women readers are always asking themselves, 'Am I normal? Oh God, my breasts are sagging.'" They want to know, she said, how they measure up with their peers, and they want solid, practical information.

❦ ❦ ❦

When you're searching for women to write about, look for someone who could be your reader's neighbor. Better still, look for your reader herself. The 1980s are over. We're past the decade of the perfect woman. We don't believe she exists. So bring on someone like us, a woman who occasionally yells at her kids, crabs at her husband and lets her house go to hell. We'll share her struggles and triumph with her when she, ultimately, gets up the next morning to plug in the coffee pot.

While women's stories are as individual as the women themselves, there are a few themes that serve to anchor them.

Remember the scene from *The Graduate* when the graying executive cornered Dustin Hoffman and whispered into his ear, "I just have one word for you, my boy...plastics." The one word I have for you in writing women's stories is: relationships. And I mean all kinds, from friends to lovers to spouses, to the delivery man who slips your pooch a treat, to the comfort level you enjoy inside your own skin.

Ten years ago an editor of the *Washington Post Magazine* advised a group of writers to open their eyes to all the relationship stories begging to be written. Specifically, those telling of women's friendships.

These relationships have become central to women's lives, maybe out of necessity. When I was a child, my mother and I visited my aunt and cousins every week—just to catch up on the news. But now, like many others, I live states away from blood family, so I seek intimacy wherever I can find it. For me, it's friends. For others, it's neighbors or causes. Notice all the articles in the 90s about building community.

Linda Wagner-Martin in *Telling Women's Lives* sees four other common themes in women's stories: a woman striving to be an individual; a woman struggling to fit into her family and community; a woman balancing the demands of her family with her own needs; and society's reaction to a woman's ambition.

When you start writing, these themes can lead you to popular stories. But soon you'll see that some of the best ideas refuse to be shoehorned into any mold. Stories emerging from these ideas spread their words freely over the rich terrain of a woman's inner life. Any story worth writing spends some time poking around and hanging out in this complex, compelling nook.

One tool to pick and probe is the past. Personal histories are incredibly important to women. How she spent yesterday shapes how she spends today, which shapes how she'll spend tomorrow. Discover who and what is relevant to her—and why. Maybe it's a mentoring aunt or a heartbreaking first love or the still stinging memories of rejection as an awkward adolescent. If it affects how she lives her life today, it's important to her story. When you look beyond the woman herself, to her family, her home, her past, you'll see things you could never imagine if you only looked straight into her eyes.

The Very First Time

OFTEN AT THE END OF A WRITING SEMINAR, a woman will come up to me and ask, "What was it like your first time?"

It's moments like these that I'm glad I'm not teaching sex ed. Actually, there are some like comparisons between my first break into a major magazine and the other first break, so to speak.

What this wistful student is asking is, how did it happen? And more important, how did it feel? She wants to live vicariously in another writer's moment, to luxuriate in the glory of big time publication when everything's gone right. And then she wants to know, step-by-step, how I pulled it off so she, too, can experience such nirvana. So here it is, no holds barred.

To begin, I remember The Call very clearly. Actually, I didn't receive it, Allen did. I was visiting my parents for the weekend in Connecticut and when I phoned home Friday night Allen said, "An editor from *Family Circle* called, and she wants to give you an assignment." Let me say here that Allen was not impressed.

"What?" I screeched. "Are you sure she said 'assignment?' Tell me word for word what she said."

That was the joy, probably the most joy I'd feel for nearly a year. But I'm getting ahead of myself.

The story was about Cathy Cook, a Connecticut mother of a Down syndrome child, who began a job training program for retarded adults. Cathy opened a bakery where the employees, all with varying degrees of mental retardation, were trained in different jobs, depending on their capabilities.

How did I get the idea? Wish I could tell you it was a reward for being a great sleuth of story ideas. Actually, it was Allen's idea. Cathy's crew catered his college reunion dinner in New England that fall and he, not me, (helps to have a sharp spouse, I guess) observed that the dinner for a few hundred guests was prepared and served by employees with Down syndrome. "Wouldn't it make a good story?" Allen persisted. I pooh-poohed his invasion into my territory, thinking of all the reasons editors wouldn't want it. Then I stored it somewhere in my brain.

As luck would have it, *Family Circle* was preparing to launch its "Women Who Make A Difference" column when my proposal to write the story—called a query letter in writing parlance—landed on the editor's desk. This high-profile column would feature ordinary women who did extraordinary things for their community. Later I'd observe *Family Circle*, more than any other magazine, has a soft spot for children with disabilities.

I know what you're thinking: perfect timing. Also, perfect persistence. I'd been submitting ideas for two years. How do I know for sure? Two years earlier, we moved from New Hampshire to our new home outside of Annapolis. No sooner had we planted the last arborvitae than Allen was assigned to be commanding officer of a ship out of Cape May, New Jersey. With our sons, 12, 10 and 6, and a menagerie of three dogs and two cats, I'd cocooned. So we decided Allen would become, as they say in the military, "a geographic bachelor," commuting home every weekend for half the year when the ship was in port. That left me lots of quiet nights to indulge my passion to beat the odds, break through the slush pile of unsolicited queries and make it happen. I was 36 and had tried my hand at being Martha Stewart back in New England. Could 40 be far ahead? While I was still a sucker for stripping old pine buried beneath coats of white paint, the time had come for me to write.

So I made a deal with myself—I do this often and highly recommend it. Two years. I'd give myself the 24 months Allen was assigned to this ship to break into a magazine one's mother-in-law could find halfway across the country. One that affords bragging rights.

Now let me run with this thought. There is nothing wrong with writing for small magazines or newspapers—at first. They're great training grounds, especially if you have a sharp editor who allows you to develop your voice while holding out a safety net if you turn into a woman who writes with the wolves. But there comes a time when you should thank your first editors for those tender bylines, and, with a fistful of clippings from your published pieces, move on to more challenging and better paying publications. Here's the catch: The time is never going to *feel* right. What insecure (and who isn't) writer, is going to wake up some morning *feeling* like she wants to trade the praise and regular publication she now gets from local editors for the uncertain, more competitive world of larger magazines and newspapers?

It doesn't matter. Just do it, one story idea at a time. Sometimes breaking into the Seven Sisters magazines—*Family Circle, Woman's Day, Ladies' Home Journal, Good Housekeeping, McCall's, Redbook* and *Better Homes and Gardens*—or other top publications, doesn't have to be a sweaty, heart-pounding workout. With the right idea and presentation, you're on your way.

So it was nearly two years to the day that *Family Circle's* fateful call came heralding my first big break. Sure I'd had other assignments. My feature articles were appearing in service club magazines like *The Optimist* and inspirational and religious magazines. Again, great break-in ground, but nothing to shine off the newsstand in Fargo.

When the *Family Circle* assignment was confirmed, I was ecstatic and told everyone, even people I didn't like. This was a big, very big mistake. Let me tell you my version of Murphy's Law. When an assignment works and even makes it to the cover, like a certain *Reader's Digest* story I can think of, absolutely no one, not even your mother, remembers it's coming out. When the magazine is finally on the newsstand you wait, but no one calls, so you call them and subtly mention how you have to find a place for the complimentary copies the editor sent you.

"Oh, what story was that now?" they ask. So you tell them. Weeks later, they tell you they couldn't find it anywhere. *Reader's Digest* goes around the world, but apparently no copies make it to my hometown of Fairfield, Connecticut, forty minutes from Manhattan. Finally you break down—writers have no pride—and you send them the blasted copy. That's why it's especially dangerous to write for third-tier, low-pay, no-prestige magazines, because if you have friends and family like mine, you'll end up spending more money sending them the darn magazines than what you earn. (Of course you can make photocopies, but you want them to see it in its full regalia, cover photos of dripping chocolate desserts juxtaposed to diet promotions.)

Let the assignment flop, your fault or fate's, and everyone, and I do mean everyone, you ever uttered a syllable to, will be asking you—for years—what happened to that story.

If you're an optimist, go ahead and broadcast your assignment, just don't let this add to the pressures of writing it.

With my *Family Circle* contract in hand, I trekked, on their expense account, to Groton, Connecticut, and spent a full day interviewing Cathy, touring the bakery and speaking with some of the employees. I felt very professional with my mini recorder (of course you should always use one) and leather attaché, although, looking back, I realize I had little notion of what I was after.

Back home I sat down to write. I was so consumed with the magnitude of the job—my words being read by millions of readers around the country—I turned catatonic. There, with furrowed brow, I worried every word that crept out of my Commodore 64 and dot matrix printer. With no idea where the story was going, worse yet, not a clear concept of what the story was really about, I was sure this was my one and only chance to prove to Miss McNally, my third grade teacher who thought I asked silly questions, how wrong she was. (Later I would learn that no matter how long it takes to get that first break, the second comes sooner.)

I'd always had an eye for drama, so I opened the piece with the most heart-wrenching, attention-grabbing anecdote.

> **When Cathy Cook gave birth to her second son, Caleb, no one sent flowers. The only acknowledgment of the 6-pound, 7-ounce baby's arrival was a letter from a friend bordered in black. Caleb was born with Down syndrome.**

From there, the story deflated. I agonized over every line, every word, every syllable, until the flow was sucked dry. The staccato rhythm, noun, verb, object, was wound as tightly as my nerves.

I'd read and reread the piece again and again until, as I know now, I wasn't hearing it anymore. Still, as I tucked it in the mail, the whole post office cheered. I was certain only time separated me from the Pulitzer prize.

For weeks I dreamed of the accolades that would come, second, third assignments. There would be no end to my success. Then the editor called. "We've got problems," she whined. I felt held hostage by the phone. She wasn't sure what was wrong, it just wasn't working. "Rewrite it," she said, offering few specifics.

I sequestered myself in my study, which resembled my emotional state: crumpled notes, ripped papers strewn everywhere, half empty cans of Diet Coke and penicillin-growing fruit. "Don't touch a thing," I'd shout, if anyone attempted to straighten up.

I was glued to every quote, every fact, every statistic. I'd become a quick expert on Down syndrome, volunteer work, small businesses, even the Nutmeg State itself. You name it, I knew it. Still, I researched more, convinced somewhere deep down that if I worked hard enough I'd be rewarded. I'm Catholic you know.

Two weeks to rewrite. I felt like I was in a steel cylinder with air being sucked out by the hour. Deadline day I crawled to the post office after hours. The next few days I avoided eye contact with others at the mall or supermarket; suddenly I didn't want to talk about this story that hung in limbo. My solace was whispered conversations with my writing friend, Karen.

A week later, the editor phoned again. Loud and clear she proclaimed, "It's even worse." I wanted to hang up but I was afraid to. I imagined the whole New York publishing world talking about just how awful my story was and chastising this editor for being so foolish to give me the assignment. I could hear the editorial staff at the magazine saying, "You mean we wasted $400 in kill fees, plus expenses?" Or worse, they were reading the piece out loud, laughing.

Realizing that I'd missed half of what the editor had said, I tried to tune in. But I feared her words. I felt like I was back in third grade

> 🐭 *Watching her move one paragraph up and another down I could feel something akin to magic: the birth of a story that would move its readers. I wrote fast, not wanting to miss a thing. I was in awe.*

and Miss McNally was passing back the tests on long division. I knew I'd failed, but maybe it wouldn't really be so if I just didn't look at the paper.

Sensing my discomfort, the editor softened, telling me we'd work on it. She ordered me to grab a pen. (These essential writer's tools are never around when editors phone.) "I'll walk you through it, point by point," she promised.

She began surgery on the piece, beginning with what the story was all about. No, not the story line about a Connecticut mother who began a bakery where she taught adults with mental retardation skills they could use in work throughout New England—but the heart of the story. The part that answers the reader's "So what? Why am I reading this story now?" The part that puts the human dimension on the facts.

"This story is about a mother's vision," the editor began. "A vision that adults with Down syndrome don't have to spend their days performing mindless tasks like pushing wooden pegs into a board. They can perform challenging work and become contributing members of the community."

"Sounds good to me," I thought.

Then she went on, "This vision of Cathy's was fueled by her experience with her own child, Caleb. Everyday this young son was passing the milestones she set for him and challenging limits that society placed on children with Down syndrome."

"Great," I said to myself. "Now how do I pull it off?"

"I'm not a great writer," she confessed, "but I'm wonderful with structure." She moved my dramatic lead down four paragraphs and in its place set the mood with a sensual description of the New England bakery complete with "the aroma of fresh-baked breads and cakes."

Watching her move one paragraph up and another down I could feel something akin to magic: the birth of a story that would move its readers. I wrote fast, not wanting to miss a thing. I was in awe.

From the lead she segued into the start of the nut (story in a nut shell) paragraph. The words flowed from her lips. I was spellbound.

> But this is no ordinary bakery. The first clue is the courteous young saleswoman carefully counting out your change. You can't help noticing her high, flat forehead and sloping eyebrows, the unnatural roundness of her face. In fact, almost everyone behind the counter has these same telltale features. They all have Down syndrome or some form of mental retardation.

Then she hit the reader hard with the perspective, the big picture.

> For these workers, mixing cake batter and serving customers is the opportunity of a lifetime. Here, thanks to Seabird Enterprises, Inc.—South East (Connecticut) Association Building Independence for the Retarded and Disabled—located in Groton, they are not only earning regular salaries and gaining useful job skills, but perhaps even more important, they are also learning self-sufficiency—and self-respect.
>
> This innovative program for mentally handicapped adults is the brainchild of one woman: Cathy Cook.

Here she inserted my original lead, the part about Caleb's birth and the way no one knew how to react.

Next she showed the reader Cathy's growing concern that no matter how much she and her family loved Caleb, the world that was waiting for him as an adult was grim. But she held out hope with the knowledge that something very strange but wonderful was happening.

> Every day Cathy saw Caleb surpassing the conventional stereotypes of a child with Down syndrome. Through early intervention, including speech and occupational therapy, and her own encouragement, Caleb was walking and talking earlier than predicted. Watching Caleb convinced Cathy that the techniques that were working with him could work for adults too.

Ah ha, the editor made the all-important leap between Caleb and Cathy's creation of the bakery.

"Now take the reader by the hand and lead her on a journey, one filled with peaks and valleys," she said. "Let the reader share Cathy's emotions as she sought funding, the frustrations she felt as she fought to convince others to share her dream," she told me. "After that, move to the next hurdle: how to teach these special employees. Include specifics like 'a non-reading student follows a picture recipe in order to mix a cake batter.'"

Throughout we developed the story's natural drama.

> The first year the bakery lost $40,000 and when Cathy closed shop on Christmas Eve 1984 she feared it might be forever. But eventually Seabird did so well, many students graduated from its bakery into local businesses including JC Penney's, the Seaport Museum, even a day care center.

At the end, we circled back to tell of Caleb, age 10, being integrated into many classes at the neighborhood school and having chores like any other child.

> Every mother is concerned about what lies ahead for her children. Thanks to Cathy Cook, the future for Caleb and for countless other retarded children looks a lot brighter.

I was grateful to the editor for saving my story, but at the same time I felt wholly inadequate.

When the September 1, 1988 issue arrived, and I saw the article for the first time, with color photos of Cathy, her family and Seabird workers, I was proud of the story, but I felt like I didn't deserve the byline. I recognized some of my original passages between smoother prose. My quotes no longer stood alone but instead were set up with a line or two of perspective. The editor also added a few lines that were judgmental; conclusions of her own.

Soon I'd receive a manila folder from her with several copies of the article and a cheery note saying "Congratulations, the piece looks great."

A few months later I opened my mail and there was a check from *Reader's Digest*; they were reprinting the story. When the *Digest* published the piece, my original lead— remember the one that began *When Cathy gave birth to her second son, Caleb, no one sent flowers*—was their lead.

Later I'd realize that any writer who puts herself into a piece to the degree I had on that one deserves her name on it.

Still I didn't dare query *Family Circle* for two years. This was a mistake. Sure, I had a lot to learn, but I had learned from that first go-round. They weren't harboring dark evil thoughts about the experience; I was doing that to myself. When I sent the second idea, they took it. The journey to publication was smoother, and I was smarter the second time around.

Ideas

ASK ANY WRITER HOW SHE GETS HER IDEAS and her answer is almost always the same, "Ideas are everywhere." Everywhere for her maybe, but for you, struggling for your first hit, her words are as satisfying as a Slim Fast shake when you're expecting shrimp with lobster sauce.

Writers who work for their ideas get published. This runs contrary to the image of a writer identifying faces in the cumulus clouds as she waits for inspiration to strike. Instead a writer who is serious about getting published fills her days with interesting stuff. She reads poetry, best-sellers, the classics, the *Wall Street Journal*, she sees movies, haunts museums, rescues orphan dogs, plants gardens, comforts the lonely. She collects experiences that fill her psyche with emotions and define her thoughts. In turn, she uses these emotions and well-shaped thoughts to develop ideas.

Here's a rundown of some ideas I've had—both winners and losers—and how I came up with them.

Let's start with an idea so strong a chimpanzee tethered to a word processor could have pulled it off. The drama featured a toddler lost in the Arizona desert for four days. The child was found just in the nick of time by a volunteer who searches for missing persons with her German shepherd.

Anyone who knows anything about readers of women's stories will spot this idea as a can't-miss. You've got a dog. You've got a baby. And you've got life and death drama.

Editors agreed. "Child Lost in the Desert" was a *Reader's Digest* cover story and their most widely read "Drama in Real Life" in five years.

How I found the idea is good news for you. An editor didn't phone with it, nor did a well-connected friend whisper it into my ear. I have no well-connected friends. The sad thing is, my friends consider *me* their well-connected friend. The moral: You don't need an uncle with a foul-smelling cigar to open editorial doors for you. You do need initiative and a generous phone budget.

I sat down on a Monday morning and actually said out loud to myself and Bargher, my tortoiseshell cat, and Charles, my black and white cat, that I was going to come up with a great idea in one week, five working days. Looking back I realize that statement was loaded with a one-two psychological punch. First, there was positive thinking: "I am going to come up with a great idea." This sentence acknowledged that there are great ideas out there, waiting to be plucked. And the second part, "I'm giving myself one week," jolted my naturally lethargic subconscious into action. Nothing like a deadline to inspire productivity.

So then what?

I skimmed *The Yearbook of Experts, Authorities and Spokespersons*, one of my freelance bibles. The *Yearbook* resembles a large city phone book. It lists experts according to topic and again according to proper name.

Experts range from internationally known doctors to the Migickian of the Holy Order of the Winged Disk of the International Academy of Hermetic Knowledge. Topics included on the D page are: DWI, dance videos, date rape, day spa salons, deafness, deal makers, death, debts, decision making, decorating, deep space networks (whatever that is), deer tick control, defense electronics and on and on. The experts pay to be listed so they're anxious to speak with you. The book is free to freelancers, call: (800) Yearbook (932-7266) for a copy of the current issue. Or find the same information at *Yearbook's* searchable website: http://www.yearbooknews.com.

Wondering what group might be privy to dramas in real life, à la *Reader's Digest* style, I came upon the National Search and Rescue League. Phoning their headquarters, I spoke with their public information spokesperson. She offered me a story about a cub scout troop lost in the mountains for a week. Sounded good. But I still asked if she had anything else and this is when she remembered the toddler and the dog.

A *Digest* editor had spelled out the guidelines for their dramas for me. For instance, the trauma couldn't end too quickly. A split second crisis won't work unless the subject's agony can be protracted. There must be enough to milk. Uh-huh. This drama took four days.

Next point. The main character, the one who is in the mess, can not be stupid. Repeat. This person must be a sympathetic character. If you're writing about a hiker freezing to death on a mountainside and the reader learns the hiker's wearing only Eddie Bauer sweats in mid-January, she's not going to care a whole lot what happens to that person. However, in the missing toddler story, reader sympathy seemed a given. A baby is always innocent, but was his mother negligent? A quick call to the mother reminded me that any reader who has cared for a child under 3 could empathize with how quickly he or she could slip away. (For the complete *Reader's Digest* drama formula, see page number 111.)

Let's go on to another idea. When an editor from *Family Circle* asked me to come up with a reunion story that was different from all the other blood, sweat and tear joinings that were all over the talk shows, I again turned to the *Yearbook* and asked myself, "Who would know about reunions?" Private detectives. I phoned six listed there, asking them for their best stories. Some got back to me with blatantly self-serving tales of tracking deadbeat dads whom others had written off. The story I was looking for would focus on a woman who struggled to find her family.

Norma Tillman, a private investigator in Nashville, told me about one woman's 23-year search to find her sister who was taken from the family as an infant. This woman devoted her life to finding her sibling, scouring the country, sleeping in cars, eating dinner out of cans. Meanwhile, the missing sister, too, was searching. Both women felt incomplete until Norma reunited them. The intensity of the story—a journey that lasted nearly a quarter of a century—made the story special. The hint of rural, southern baby-snatching boosted its strength. The idea was assigned.

Still another time I sat down with the *Yearbook* and a Diet Coke and participated in a right-brain exercise. I asked myself what type of stories do I like to write? Relationship pieces. So flipping through the pages I noted groups and individuals who might offer leads to such stories. One such group was Big Brothers/Big Sisters of America, headquartered in Philadelphia. At first their spokesperson fed me ideas ideal for a local or regional publication, but not rich enough for a national magazine. I emphasized that the story I was seeking would be deeper, fuller, more significant, a story that readers across the country would care about—even if they never heard of the subject's hometown.

"We've got a Big Sister who rescued her Little Sister from a life of abuse," the public relations type continued. "The Little Sister is now ready to enter law school and their 14-year relationship is still strong. But that story is out in Los Angeles."

"No problem," I blurted gratefully.

A writer is never restricted to an area code.

When you're sleuthing for stories, a few dollars more in a phone bill often results in a profitable assignment. It makes it easier to come up with powerful stories if your hunting ground is the entire country, or even the globe.

I knew I'd hit pay dirt with this story, so I asked for details. Fourteen years of an abused child's life was a gold mine for drama. At one point, the child's home life became so unbearable that she moved in with her Big Sister, an act the organization does not encourage. Now with the Big Sister thrust in the disciplinarian role, their friendship was jeopardized. Great material. The story was assigned.

Another idea that worked was the story of Janice DeBlois who reared her blind, autistic son Tony to become a musical savant. How did I find this story? Profnet. Profnet is an on-line service linking more than 25,000 public information specialists from colleges and universities, public relations agencies and corporations across the country with writers seeking stories. Usually writers use it for specific information, or for story background. But you can use your feminine (or masculine) wiles to make it work even harder for you.

Here's what I do. I submit a broad topic and see what develops. For instance, I found Janice's story after submitting a Profnet request for outstanding college graduates. A public relations person from Berklee College of Music in Boston, where Tony was graduating, saw my request and phoned. I sent him clips and he agreed to give me three weeks to get a contract on the story, before he would offer it to others. The story was timely because of the graduation.

I faxed several magazines queries. An editor from *Life* magazine responded two days later and I had a contract within a week. (Faxing story ideas is usually not a good idea. Most editors say they prefer the postal service, others reserve their faxing and electronic mail for their regular writers. But I considered this a special situation. Never be afraid to break the rules.)

Profnet is free to writers making requests. The public information specialists pay to receive our questions.

To submit a query to Profnet call 1-(800) Profnet (776-3638). Be sure to include the publications you're targeting and the deadline for replies, plus how you prefer to be contacted. If you wish certain information, such as the name of a magazine, kept confidential, it can be cloaked for general calls and revealed only to those Profnet members who respond positively.

The service's list is segmented and you may ask that your query only be broadcast to one or a combination of the following five lists: colleges and universities; extended academe (the foregoing plus think tanks, national labs and scientific associations); corporations and public relations agencies; nonprofit organizations and government agencies. If one query doesn't draw, you can ask that it be redirected, or rewrite your request. If you are overwhelmed with responses and want to turn it off, the service will do just that. It will even post your thank-you notes.

More ways to find experts:

Profnet Experts Database is a website offering profiles of 2,000 individuals identified as leaders in their fields; it's at www.profnet.com.

MediaResource Service focuses on finding interviewees with varying viewpoints in science, medicine and technology and can be helpful as an additional resource in those subject areas. Its modus operandi is similar to Profnet's. Phone MRS at (800) 223-1730 or go to www.mediaresource.org on the internet.

BizNews works similarly, helping to ferret out sources in the business world; contact by e-mail, rjohnson@newswise.com or on the web at www.newswise.com.

PartyLine is a weekly newsletter for more leisurely deadlines such as a book or a column. For information e-mail info@partyline publishing.com, or go to website: www.party line publishing.com.

🍎 As you start to pay attention to published stories, you'll detect a certain something about them, a fullness, a completion, diverse concepts making the whole greater than the sum of the parts.

One last winning idea and then we'll turn to the losers.

Driving my youngest son Ryan to school one morning after he'd missed the bus, we passed a trailer park. "That's where my friend Lacey lives," Ryan remarked.

"Hmmmm," I mumbled, wondering how fast I could get him to school and return home to my writing.

"Lacey is having his third open heart surgery soon," Ryan continued. "That would be a good story for you, Mom."

"What a shame, Ryan, I hope Lacey will be feeling better soon," I said, still thinking about my work.

"Why don't you write about him?"

"Lacey's story might make a good article for *The Capital* (our local paper), but not a larger publication," I explained.

"But Mom," Ryan persisted. "Lacey's brother, Gary, who's 11, has a dozen cancerous brain tumors, and one's the size of an orange."

If I hadn't known Ryan, I'd think my child was swimming in the grotesque.

"Oh, Ryan that's awful," I said. "I don't know when I've heard of anything so sad. Let's think about what we can do to help them." By now my concern was genuine.

"Well, do you want to do the story?"

"Ryan, that's the saddest story I've heard in a long time, but I just don't think it's for me," I said gently. "It doesn't have a point."

"But Mom," Ryan continued, undeterred. "Their mother left them a long time ago and their dad's been taking care of them all by himself."

Now *there* was the story. That one detail elevated this tragic saga into something more. Something that would move readers.

As you start to pay attention to published stories, you'll detect a certain something about them, a fullness, a completion, diverse concepts making the whole greater than the sum of the parts. When you recognize this something extra in potential stories, you'll experience an adrenaline flush—an epiphany—that will drive you to your word processor to knock out that query letter.

Family Circle published "Father Love" in June 1992, and reader response was overwhelming. The family received cash, toys, clothing, child care, even oceanfront vacations. A young woman by the name of Gabrielle, waiting to board a plane in Boston to fly to New York on business, picked up the magazine. Reading the story, she was so touched she phoned Gary from the airport. Soon she flew to meet him and the boys, and within a few months moved to Maryland to help care for the family. Eventually Gary proposed to her.

If you are wondering why Ryan was so intent on finding a story, let me reveal that I bribe everyone I know to come up with winning ideas in exchange for a finder's fee of 10 percent of what I'm paid for the piece.

So much for the winners. Now let's consider the also-rans and what they can teach us.

One of my first queries told of our oldest son Scott's eye injury. *Ladies' Home Journal* asked to see the story on speculation.

You write on speculation, if asked, when you're new to a publication and don't have clips from other newspapers or magazines of similar stature. Speculation means the editor risks nothing—not even the small "kill fee" (usually 20 percent of the contracted price for a piece) normally offered with an assignment. Writing on speculation gives a new writer a chance to break into a publication. But once you've earned your clippings of published pieces, tell editors who ask you to write on spec—ever so kindly—thank you, but no thank you.

I considered Scott's injury a heart-tugging, vital drama. I explained how Scott and a classmate, Jason, both 10, had just begun playing with new tennis rackets in the sand outside our rented beach home. Jason volleyed the ball and Scott missed. As Scott bent to retrieve it, Jason— not meaning any malice—took a rock and hit it with the racket. The two children were about four feet apart when the rock hit Scott in his left eye. The story explained how Scott suffered a traumatic cataract and had to have the lens in his eye removed. Worse yet, the rock caused retina damage in the macula, or fine vision area. His eyesight could never be restored to normal.

I wrote the story to alert readers to the seriousness of eye injuries and the importance of protection, even for games like tennis.

The story was rejected with no explanation. My writing at that time may not have been up to the *Journal's* standards. It's also possible that as traumatic as the incident was for me, it was not life-threatening, so it paled as a drama. And since I didn't delve into lots of information on eye injuries and protective gear, it didn't work as a service piece either. (A service piece is one of those popular article types that teaches the reader something to help her live better, whether it's beating stress, saving money, cooking up low-cal desserts, expanding her creativity— or keeping her kids safe from eye injuries.)

A few years later I used the material in an essay on the vulnerability of motherhood, exploring how we, too, suffer the arrows that pierce our children's lives.

Another story that never found a home came to me from a media representative from Johns Hopkins Children's Center in Baltimore. She alerted me to a family living a half hour away who had adopted a child with the birth defect ambiguous genitalia, or unclear sexual identity. The family thought they were bringing home a Korean daughter and instead they became parents to a son. Handled insensitively, this could be a tabloid sensation. But set in the framework of a family with seven adopted Korean children with special physical or mental needs, the picture that develops is as heartwarming as the Waltons.

The mother and father were willing to explore with candor their son's medical condition and their own hopes and fears because they thought that the more the public knew about the condition the less taboo it would seem. I would support their story with the expertise of Johns Hopkins doctors. While ambiguous genitalia is a rare defect, I thought it was intriguing, especially with the wonders of modern surgery.

I considered the story perfect for *Family Circle* and envisioned a full page photo of this attractive family: thirty-something, blond parents intertwined with seven raven-haired, olive skinned smiling children, steps apart in size. I was already blocking out time to write the story when the editor phoned.

"Yuk," was her reaction.

"What?" I couldn't believe my ears. I considered the story worthy of a bidding war.

"It's just too weird," she said.

She'd missed the point, I was sure, so I set it up again.

"Our readers wouldn't like it."

That's the key. No matter how compelling an idea is, a good editor knows her readers and if an article or story doesn't fit them, it doesn't work for the magazine—no matter what.

Oddly enough all but one of the other editors I queried, and you *know* I hit them all, had the same reaction. (Maybe you do too.) Still I was shocked. You mean in a country where the president is accused of dropping his pants to a state worker, readers would be repulsed by the story of a child whose genitals were not fully developed at birth?

Finally *Redbook* phoned. "We're interested. Will you write it on spec?"

"You've got to be joking!" I exclaimed.

Did I really say that? Close to it. By then I'd collected a fistful of clips from magazines with circulations larger than *Redbook's*. If this magazine couldn't risk a few hundred dollars in a kill fee if the story didn't work, I couldn't risk my time.

They didn't budge and neither did I.

What can we conclude about this idea? Editors want ideas that are a tinge beyond the ordinary, but not so far from the center that readers can't relate. And in our seemingly shockproof society, there are still subjects that, to some readers, are taboo.

As a final also-ran idea, an article titled "Letting Go of Erin" in our local paper told of a baby boomer mom who devoted the past 21 years to caring for her severely deformed daughter. Never out of earshot of this girl, the two molded into one. After months of painful soul searching, the mother placed her daughter in a home where professionals would care for her. The article told of the adjustment both women had to make when they broke their incredibly tight bond. The narrative ended with the mom watching her daughter forge an independent life.

When I pitched a story on this mother-daughter saga, the editors all had the same reaction: "Too sad." Times eight.

Now let's take a look at ideas with circuitous paths to publication.

At the end of a writing seminar in Los Angeles a few years ago, a young blond woman with a generous smile came up to me and introduced herself as Kathy Scobee Fulgham. Offering her hand and smiling she said, "You probably don't remember the name, but my dad was Dick Scobee, the mission commander of the Challenger space shuttle."

Suddenly I remembered the image of her on television, sitting beside her mother at the Challenger memorial service days after the shuttle exploded into national tragedy. The two teary-eyed women stared into the sky as the Air Force jets blasted overhead in the missing-man formation.

She explained that she and her mother were writing a coffee table type book commemorating the ten-year anniversary of the Challenger explosion and could I advise her about getting an agent.

After telling her what I knew, I asked if she and her mother might consider allowing me to write a magazine article about them for the occasion.

"Sure," she replied.

The anniversary was 18 months away, so I made a note to contact them in six months. Then I wrote Kathy and her mother, June Scobee, sending both my clips of published articles and asking for their story.

They phoned enthusiastically ready to begin. I focused my query on how mother and daughter helped one another out of the depths of despair. Because of the anniversary, the story idea was an easy sell to *Woman's Day*.

Even more interesting is the spin-off from this story. In querying about the Scobees, I offered a sidebar. A sidebar is the short secondary story, usually set apart from the main story in the layout by a box or other graphic design. This sidebar would track what had become of the other Challenger families.

When I phoned Christa McAuliffe's mother, Grace Corrigan, she spoke so openly that I realized this was another story, not just a sidebar. And, as the mother of the Challenger's most beloved traveler, this was the more important story. Midway through our conversation, I asked if she'd be willing to have a story written about her and she agreed. I sent the query to *Family Circle* as my gift for all the lessons they've taught me.

What keeps freelancing fascinating are the surprises and this idea was no exception. The editor phoned and in an incredulous tone explained that her boss said, "Thanks, but we'll pass." I was left shaking my head. Could it be that they considered the story too celebrity-oriented? As it turned out, six months later they asked if it was still available but it had been scooped up by *McCall's*.

Backpeddling some, let me say that I sensed this story was too important to languish in a slush pile of freelance submissions until it made some first-reader's day. So when *Family Circle* turned it down, I broke all the rules and called *McCall's*. Not knowing anyone there, I asked for any editor. A young man came to the phone, asked what the idea was and if I could fax him the query along with clips.

Minutes later he phoned with questions: How did I get the story? Was I certain we could obtain the exclusive? "Sit tight," he said. "Give me just a little time to present it to my editor." Because I was sure this idea was a winner, I did not shop it around. He phoned again in two days assigning the story, but he wanted it structured differently.

"Lessons Christa Taught Us," the original focus of the feature became its sidebar. "The Whole World Loved My Daughter" was written in a first person, as-told-to format, as if Mrs. Corrigan herself were speaking. The blurb read, "Since the space shuttle Challenger exploded and claimed Christa McAuliffe's life ten years ago, Grace Corrigan has become proof that ordinary people can do extraordinary things." *McCall's* considered Grace's personal journey since her daughter's death to be the real story—and rightly so.

I learned another lesson in how editors choose story ideas. A *McCall's* editor phoned asking me to come up with some ideas on animals that would prove the ever-deepening bond between people and pets. I began by phoning the public relations people from the Delta Society, the American Humane Society, PAWS with a Cause and others. Within a week I wrote a thumbnail sketch of six suggestions. A week later the editor assigned two of my ideas and gave me one of his own.

❦ ❦ ❦

Let's see if you think like an editor. Pretend you are a *McCall's* editor. Remember your readers are somewhat independent women who are fairly well-educated. Now decide which of these two ideas you'd select.

Idea number one

Bruno is one of the few dogs in this country who serves as both the eyes of his mistress—a blind and beautiful 33-year-old California lawyer—and as her service companion. Besides being sightless since age 9, Natalie Wormeli uses a wheelchair because of multiple sclerosis.

After graduating from the University of California at Davis School of Law in 1993, Natalie found herself practicing out of her home—but not by choice. The few job interviews she went on left her pale. "They began with me being wheeled in like a hospital patient," she says. "That's a tough first impression to overcome." Reluctantly Natalie retreated to her apartment.

Then, one November, all that changed—thanks to a 95-pound yellow Labrador retriever named Bruno. Bruno is trained to perform both guide dog and service dog tasks. He leads Natalie across busy intersections, pulls her wheelchair up ramps, even presses the elevator buttons to her office floor—quite a feat for a worker who asks only for an occasional pat on the head.

"It's overwhelming how he's changed my life," says Natalie. From day one the two worked as a team. Natalie gives a command and Bruno follows it. She holds Bruno's harness with one hand and grabs onto the chair with the other. She compares the ride to water skiing single-handed.

Today Natalie's still practicing law, but she's no longer working from home. Instead, like many others, she commutes to work, joining her colleagues at the office. Getting out of the house is just the beginning for Natalie and Bruno. Says she, "Watch out world, here we come, a lawyer on wheels with her big dog."

Idea number two

Sherry Reif, 30, who battles multiple sclerosis, has spent much of the last five years in a wheelchair. But with the help of her service dog, a Rottweiler named Eric, she's had adventures others could hardly imagine. Consider for one, parachuting out of an airplane at 15,000 feet.

More impressive, she's happily married and rearing two children, adopted daughter Alysse, 6, and son Andy, 11. Andy was born prematurely with cerebral palsy and attends special education classes. Bringing up a family is a challenge for any parent, let alone a mother with a severe physical challenge caring for a child with one. But with the help of a companion who never balks at overtime, weekend duty, or tasks he considers beneath him, Sherry is able to be a wife, mother and homemaker.

Time's up. Which idea would you select for *McCall's*? Now for extra credit, pretend you are a *Family Circle* editor, would your decision be the same?

Ready?

Here are the real life answers.

McCall's chose the story of Natalie Wormeli because the idea was two-pronged. First there was Natalie's story of self-determination and then there was the story of a remarkable dog—the only dually-trained dog working in the country today.

Now for the extra credit question, and I warn you this is pure speculation. I think the *Family Circle* editors would probably bite on Sherry's story because she is a wife and mother and offers stronger reader identification. And with the extra dimension of a special needs mother caring for a special needs child, they just might be interested. Hmmm. I think I'll go write a query letter.

Even More Ideas

CHECK OUT OF THE LIBRARY a stack of two or three-year-old issues of a publication you plan to write for.

Scan the articles and free associate. What new ideas do these articles suggest? Consider giving a few of the topics this year's make over. Jot down notes.

Here are three ways to rethink the same old subjects.

The fresh approach

Read the article titles and blurbs in the front of the magazine. Then think how you would flesh out such stories. What angle would you take? What tone would you choose? Who would you interview? Would you include anecdotes and quotes or would you present it as a straight informative piece? Would you put your opinion in subtly, or more blatantly? Now read the story. How close did you come? If you were miles apart, whose version did you like better, the author's or yours? Would the editor have agreed? Is your new version a fresh enough idea to propose to the editor?

Take the road less written

If everyone's proposing stories about everyday women making money in neighborhood investment clubs, à la the best-seller *The Beardstown Ladies,* you suggest, "I Was An Investment Club Drop-Out."

Combine and conquer

It's tough to come up with full-feature, pulse-racing, exclusive stories every month, so think combos. A story about a woman who donates a kidney to a coworker may not be strong enough to warrant 2,000 words in a major publication, but combine that idea with two or three other profiles of "Anything for a Friend" and you've captured an editor's attention.

Juxtapose views, life-styles, anything. Try mother and daughter, city woman and country woman, liberal and conservative viewpoints on any intriguing topic.

Ideas seldom arrive hatched and ready to fly. They need you to nurture them, give them time to develop wings and, when they're ready and not a moment sooner, release them.

🐞 🐞 🐞

Besides panning for ideas for the main story, you'll want to identify thoughts for sidebars, those secondary stories that are set off from the main story by boxes, bars or some other graphic design.

Never forget that a reader reads for one reason: to gain something. Sidebars grab the reader by her nose and say, "Hey, look, here's something for you." Sidebars are your way of spotlighting a bit of easy-to-take-home information. Sidebars can be anything from a short numbered list, to a fairly comprehensive profile of something or someone. A sidebar's content is limited only by your imagination and the reader's interest. Let's look at a few recent examples.

Woman's Day featured a profile of Naomi Judd, "The Sweet Sound of Healing: Given Little Hope for a Full Recovery, the Country Star Found her Own Path to Health and Happiness." Its sidebar "Coping with Crisis" (a shaded box on the lead page) offered Naomi's three points for readers going through tough times: Be aware that you are in control, create your own reality and simplify your life. Each had a few lines of explanation in Naomi's own words.

Family Circle's "Women Who Make A Difference" column told of a woman who founded the Massachusetts Eating Disorders Association and saved a young girl's life. The drama was shored up with a two-part sidebar. The first part was titled, "11 Danger Signs" of eating disorders—information gleaned from experts, including the assistant surgeon general of the U.S. Department of Heath and Human Services. (Getting experts to contribute is usually no problem. Tell them you are writing an article for a particular publication—and, unless asked, there's no need to say you don't have the assignment, yet.)

The second part of this sidebar referred readers to three books on the topic and gave instructions on how to reach the association.

Cosmopolitan's article, "The No-Fail Guide to Getting the Ring You Want," included the sidebar "Surprise, Surprise: You Hate It"—what to do if your incurably romantic man proposes with a ring that looks like it came out of a gumball machine.

Ladies' Home Journal's holiday feature on Roma Downey, the star of "Touched by an Angel," included the sidebar "How I Became An Angel" by Downey's co-star Della Reese. The excerpt was from Reese's new autobiography *Angels Along The Way*.

Redbook's "Get the Best Maternity Leave for You (And Your Baby)" carried seven sidebars to the main story: "Family Leave: Limits of the Law"; "5 Things All Bosses Want To Hear"; "Words for Wise Negotiators"; "Tips for Pregnant Job Hunters"; "Unfair Companies: How to Fight Back"; "They're Not So Glad You're Back" and "Dream Leaves: Three Women's Stories."

Woman's Day's "Supermoms, What Are their Secrets?" was nearly all sidebars set up by a few paragraphs that presented the theme of the article. The seven sidebars included photos of mothers and their kids and tips for super families. The first few words of each mother's hint were boldfaced to engage the casual reader scanning the magazine.

Where do you get ideas for sidebars? Somewhere in your interviews or research you'll come upon material that makes you say, "Wow." You rush to tell your friends, and they're interested too. This is good stuff. If it doesn't fit in the strong focus of your feature article, all the better. Let it breathe on its own in a sidebar.

Sidebars help sell article ideas to editors because readers love them. If your research shows that the publication uses sidebars—*Vanity Fair*, for instance, seldom does—be sure to mention two or three sidebar possibilities in your query.

Massaging Ideas

BE OPEN TO THE MODIFICATION of your original idea—either on your own initiative or the editor's. Sometimes a slightly different slant, a tighter focus—or even a broader focus—may rescue an article idea.

A *Family Circle* editor was offered a query about Feng Shui, an Eastern system of managing energy flow to live a luckier, happier life. She was intrigued by the topic but sensed it would be too avant-garde for her readers. So she asked the author to write about Feng Shui but also to include more traditional methods. The title: "Boost Your Luck in Love and Money."

An unfocused, downer-type proposal suggesting a self-help article on "How to Control Your Anger" was transformed into a winning story: "How To Use Your Strongest Emotion To Improve Your Marriage." (Yes, it's anger.)

Another writer proposed an article advising readers of *Family Circle* on getting along with stepchildren. While blended families are prevalent in America, *Family Circle*'s editors were concerned the topic was too narrow so they broadened it to embrace nearly every reader. "Secrets to Happy Families" spoke to stepparenting as one of several ways to be a family.

A tight focus is often best. *Self* magazine, which deals with readers who want to change their lives, published as a monthly serial one woman's journal on living with lymphoma. Another time the editor gave an assignment to a new writer who reached deep within herself to explore "Why I Am Obsessed With Shoes."

Ladies' Home Journal receives hundreds of proposals about cancer. Much can be written about this deadly disease, but *Journal* editors would advise you to be specific. "Breast Cancer Myths Women Still Believe" was what one writer decided.

The same advice applies to the topic of money. How about, "The 5 Money Mistakes Every Woman Makes"? Or speaking of health, "5 Alternative Health Treatments that Can Do More Harm Than Good."

The *Journal* showed the power of packaging in the article titled "Is Your Husband Making You Sick?" The article rounded up studies on health habits such as snoring, alcohol abuse and secondhand smoke. Although there was nothing new in each study, gathering them together under such a compelling title won readers.

New Woman likes to push the limits with subjects such as medical intuition and new ways to heal. One attention-grabbing title they used is "Women Turned Off By Sex." Another time the magazine received a query about nuns, informing the editor that women who enter the convent today usually have led full, diversified lives before settling into a more cloistered existence. This surprised the editor who said she immediately asked herself, "Why would a woman who has been in the world give it all up?" She was baited. She knew the reader would want to know too. When she read the frank questions the writer said she would ask the nuns—and they were the same ones this editor wanted answered—she made the assignment. Ask yourself how you can push the limits on one of your article ideas.

Parade magazine took the up-close and personal approach to the broad, controversial issue of guns by publishing a woman's essay, "Why I Own A Gun." They also chose to divert from the popular point of view with their story "Emotional Abuse: You Don't have To Forgive Him."

Each of these published stories offered focus, creativity and a dollop of intrigue. Tried and true topics can work if you ask yourself what's new. Take the subject of domestic violence. Is there a current study or an avant-garde program to which it can be hitched? How about "Women Who Hit First"?

Speaking at a writers' conference, an editor gave this advice on massaging story ideas, "Remember: reader, reader, reader." Then she took the topic of sex and ran it through a woman's magazine checklist. Here's what she came up with.

> *Woman's Day*: "5 Ways to Keep Long-Term Love Exciting"
> *Working Mother*: "5 Ways to Make Time For Sex"
> *New Woman*: "5 Ways to Tell If He's Cheating"
> *Cosmopolitan*: "5 Ways to Tell If You Should Cheat"
> *Playgirl*: "5 Ways to Have A Multiple Orgasm."

Love Letters—aka Query Letters

WHEN YOU WRITE TO AN EDITOR proposing a story idea, write a love letter. Toss out the conventional notion of a query letter or proposal, and instead focus on passion, emotion, a sense of urgency, even a bit of breathlessness. Only by writing this way will you shake the editor from the stupor evoked by reading all those staid, letter-perfect proposals, proposals that go nowhere except into the rejection pile.

From the very first words of this personal letter, the editor will sense you're different from all the other hacks vying for her attention. You're on to something, and she'll notice.

Design the letter to be visually pleasing. No, don't rush out and buy a desktop publishing program with fancy fonts, graphics and logos with smiling faces. Nothing shouts amateur as loudly. Instead use a businesslike typeface. And don't cram every square inch with copy, allow sufficient white space, giving the editor, as reader, room to breathe.

Similar to any letter expressing affection, the query should connect with her on a visceral level, acknowledging that she is a person, not merely a ticket to publication. Beginning with the salutation, make her feel chosen. You've thoughtfully selected her, whether she's a senior editor or the lifestyle editor or whomever. Address her by name and spell it correctly.

Next, type your article's title, center it a few lines down from the salutation and set it off in boldface. This is the first step to help the editor envision the article in her publication.

Let me explain a little more. Visual presentation is everything that frames an article; the photos or art work, the title, the subheads (those bold face phrases that break up blocks of text), the sidebars, the boxes, even the italicized lines at the end noting reference material.

Editors love writers to supply these things because they lend themselves to creative layouts that attract readers. Surveys show that readers look at these visual elements and decide in a few seconds whether to go on to read the first paragraph or two.

Listing in your query letter the visual elements you will supply helps the editor to imagine the story in print and moves you closer to getting the assignment.

OK, now that you've written and centered your title, conjure up a coverline or two that might—if the editor deems the story enticing enough—make it to the cover of the publication. Yes, this is the editor's job. Do it for her and she will love you. She might even assign you the piece. Place the coverline below the title, centered but not boldfaced.

You've been told everywhere else to keep your query letter to one page. I swear this is a scam propagated by published writers who want to keep new ones from nipping at their assignments. True, three single-spaced pages to an editor who picks up your letter a half hour before lunch is unappetizing. But don't shortchange yourself. If you've got something to say—and you better if you're writing to her—then relax and allow yourself space to make your point. For me, one-and-a-half to two pages seems comfortable.

The lead

The main part of the letter is divided into six sections. The first is the lead, a few paragraphs with a big job. Here you choose the most compelling part of the story and breathe life into it. In a true-life drama query the lead brings the editor to the brink, the moment of crisis, then lets her hang. The query to "Leap of Faith,"—the story of two desperately ill children who were best friends and needed the same liver, began this way:

> "This is the situation," Dr. Thomas Starzl said to the two mothers waiting outside the operating room. "We've located one liver. Candi needs it, but we can stabilize her now. Jason's liver is gangrenous; he's going to die tonight unless he gets a new one."
>
> Besides everything else they had in common, the two children were about the same size and had the same blood and tissue types, making the organ suitable for either of them. Dr. Starzl believed it would only be right to give those who would be most affected by the choice a part in making it—even if that meant confronting Candi's mother with the toughest decision of her life. Turning to Penny, he asked, "What should we do?"
>
> Penny looked at Nancy, who had tears in her eyes, and wondered how she could weigh her own child's life

against another's. How could she gamble that another
liver would become available in time?

In a few lines we've gotten the editor to put down her coffee and
pay attention.

Writing friend, Lynn Gosman, began her love letter to an editor at
Ladies' Home Journal like this:

> After fifty years of marriage my mother, a vital,
> attractive, loving woman and the apple of my father's
> eye, was diagnosed with ovarian cancer. Six weeks later
> she was dead.
>
> Needless to say it was devastating to friends and
> family, but most of all to my father who after the initial
> shock soon became despondent. "There will never be
> another woman for me," he cried, as I tried in vain to
> comfort him. I understood his pain. I, too, felt the emp-
> tiness that her death had brought. How could either of
> us know in the midst of our grief that less than seven
> months later my father would be engaged? Surprised?
> So was I, since I inadvertently arranged it.

Could you stop reading? Neither could the editor.

If the story is a service piece chock-full of information, use the
lead to show the editor how the reader will be luxuriating in her new,
improved life—thanks to your article. Take a look at the lead in my
query to *Family Circle* for "Don't Pay For It—Trade For It":

> If you've ever wished upon a star, now's your
> chance. A diamond necklace, a romantic cruise, piano
> lessons, even cosmetic surgery can be yours without
> spending a dime—when you barter instead of buy.

If you're stuck for how to begin, crawl into yourself and ask, What
images come to mind? What's the story's most dramatic moment?
What's the hottest information you've got to tell? What's the first thing
you'd tell a friend about the idea? These are all triggers to possible
openers.

When writing to the editor of a facts-only type publication like
Bridal Guide, for instance, swallow your love for anecdotes and scene-
setting and launch the letter in the style she prefers, listing what's new

and relevant to readers. Your letter should demonstrate to the editor that you know her readers, intimately.

Check to be sure the tone of your writing is in tandem with the publication's. Get under your skin the subtle nuances of how the writers published in this magazine address the reader and the reader's attitude towards the subject. One big clue: Read the letters from the editor and write the way she speaks to her readers.

The middle section

In the second part of your letter, broaden your idea. It is here you convey a sense of urgency if appropriate. If your idea pivots on a hard news peg, such as the Challenger space shuttle anniversary, say so and tell how it relates to the readers. But if your piece is an evergreen, a seemingly always fresh subject, show the editor why this topic is hot with her readers and why it will be for months.

Remember, newspapers work fast—days, weeks. Regional publications take longer, one to six months from query to publication. And the nationals, well, have patience and think of Christmas ideas in May.

Now give the editor more to chew on. The second part of the transplant proposal explained that both 6-year-olds had their days marked with medications, surgeries and the uncertainties of whether they'd see their next Christmas. Now these best friends were united for an incredible fight for life. I promised the editor her readers would share the families' nail-biting tension as doctors transplant Jason and struggle to keep Candi alive while awaiting an organ for her. And every mother (yes, most of her readers are mothers) would see herself in this story and ask, "What would I do?"

The middle of Lynn's query about her dad's remarriage read:

> Yes, I introduced my father to Maryanne, a client of mine whose husband had passed away shortly before my mother. But my only thoughts were to provide him with an occasional dinner partner. Now I was plagued with guilt. Was I a traitor to my mother or a loving daughter only doing what she would have wanted me to do?
>
> Should I have told my dad, like some friends I know have done to their surviving parent, that I strongly disapproved, that I would never tolerate another person in my mother's role? Did I have the right to expect my

> father, even at the age of 75, to live the rest of his life
> alone? If not, could I hide the resentment I felt that a
> union of a half-century could be so easily replaced?

Within a week, this idea rose from the bottom of a slush pile to the top of the article editor's desk because every line was sealed with Lynn's passion.

The idea oozed with reader identification. Lynn didn't have to spell out to the editor that her readers are aging and, if they haven't yet confronted a parents' remarriage, they know they might soon.

This topic had another thing going for Lynn, if the editor liked the idea—and she did—she had to take its writer, in spite of the fact Lynn had no clips from major publications. This was Lynn's story and no one else could tell it—a great way to break in to larger newspapers and magazines.

Below is how I handled the same section of the query when I wrote about bartering. I told the editor that bartering's not new. It comes with a wonderful history. "Years ago, neighbors bargained over backyard fences—swapping quilts for homemade preserves, child care for slipcovers. Women have always been natural barterers," I assured her, "combining their skills, creativity and resourcefulness to get what they want."

What *is* new is bartering 90s style.

> Today barter is big business. More than $1 billion
> in goods and services exchanged hands last year in North
> America alone. The power of negotiation is multiplied
> many times over in homes across the country as women
> join small neighborhood clubs or one of the 600 com-
> mercial exchanges—and trade just about any service or
> product you can imagine.

If the query is full of information, pare it down. Leave only the fiery, most relevant stuff, that with life-changing potential for the reader.

When you have four or five pieces of information to get across, consider listing them in bullet form—those little typographical dots used to set off paragraphs are available now with most word processors. Bulleted paragraphs make it easy for the editor to comprehend.

The can-do section

This next section serves as a reality check. The editor will want to know if the story itself is doable. To assuage her fears, spell out exactly what you will do. Will you spend a semester in high school incognito to report on how teens have changed? Will you camp out at the pediatric emergency room of a metropolitan hospital to give an insider's view of child abuse?

Who will you interview? If the story hinges on interviews with hard-to-reach people or one-of-a-kind experts, be sure to nail them down before you approach the editor. This legwork must be done before she'll assign the story.

Tell the editor what questions you'll ask. Give her at least three or four to show her the shape your story will take. Intersperse deep, thought-provoking questions with light, frivolous ones. List questions that relate directly to the piece and a few that seem to have no connection. List a question no one else would think of asking.

If you haven't done it by now, you might want to mention where in the publication you think the idea will fit. If you're pitching for a column you note that near the title. Some writers feel pushy telling the editor where they think the article should go, as if they're telling the editor what to do. But the editors I know say they feel complimented that the writer has studied their issues.

Students often ask me how much research to put into a query. Details are important to give your story its own thumbprint, making it different from every other article that's been written on that topic. But guard against over-researching until the assignment's cinched. You need just enough to make an editor hungry.

For instance, an idea triggered by an article in a small newspaper can be fleshed out with a call to the woman involved and another one to a national expert. Use the core story as a springboard to your interpretation.

In the "Leap of Faith" proposal, I promised extensive interviews with both families and the surgeon. It was vital that I be able to speak with Dr. Starzl because he triggered the drama. There would have been no story if he hadn't asked Candi's mother which child should get the organ.

When I queried about bartering, I only told of my experience trading writing lectures for two passages on a world cruise. I knew better. But I wrote the query as Allen was loading our suitcases into the trunk. I planned on saving the rejection slip as proof that I tried to sell a story and could then claim the trip's incidental expenses as a tax write-off. This is probably the first and only time you'll hear of a writer trying to get a rejection. And wouldn't you know it, I failed.

The editor liked the idea enough to ask me to flesh it out. I rounded-up four other women around the country whose bartering skills readers would relate to. I also added a few quotes from bartering experts and a statistic showing its popularity.

The postlude

The fourth part of your letter tells the editor in a sentence or two why this story is important. You want to be sure she understands what it all means, what the point of the article is.

Reader's Digest calls this point the postlude. Feeding this to the editor often separates writers who get assignments from the wannabes. For some writers, this is the toughest part. Let's look at Lynn's query about her widowed dad's remarriage and see how she handled it.

> **Things happen, people die, relationships break up...I invite your readers to share in my voyage of reconciling the human need to remember those we love with the painful but necessary need to gravitate towards life. To come to the understanding, like me, that while their loved one is not here, opening their heart to someone new, although threatening, is worth it. Maryanne, my dad's new wife, has given us a gift that even my mother would be grateful for.**

Here is the postlude to the barter query:

> **Women throughout the country are trading their own special skills to make their dreams come true. This is a trend readers won't want to miss.**

🐨 🐨 🐨

When we get to this part in my workshops someone always asks, "What can you do to stop an editor from stealing your idea?"

I silently groan, then tell them that this should be their last concern. "Worry about writing a great query," I say. "Better yet, don't worry at all. Just get the ideas out there."

🐨 🐨 🐨

The perks

In the first part of your letter, you captured the editor's attention and drew her in. Then you showed her exactly how you would write the story and overcame any hesitations she harbored about whether the idea was workable. You followed this by telling her why the story was important. Now, in part five, you entice her even more, mentioning any perks that ante up the story's appeal.

In a query about a story out of Los Angeles, I said I was giving a seminar in that city and the magazine could save on air fare. The editor quickly assigned the story. Although she had a full inventory for the column, she couldn't resist a bargain.

When I wrote about 12-year-old Richie, who was killed riding his bike to school, I noted that his sixth-grade journal was open to us. Special photos of Challenger Commander Dick Scobee and his family were offered to *Woman's Day*.

While we all want to be assigned a full feature for the well, or middle section of the magazine, wouldn't a 300-word quickie in the front be better than a rejection? It "breaks" you in at the magazine and gives you a byline to mention. This is the place in the query to offer secondary or shorter angles for the idea. It's also the time to suggest topics for sidebars or boxes. But keep this limited. You don't want to divert the editor's attention from the main idea.

This is also the place to say how photogenic your subject and her family are—if it's true.

Why me?

The sixth and final part of the love letter is the toughest. Here you hone in why you're the perfect writer for the piece. You spotlight what you've done and let your passion ooze off the page.

This isn't easy. If you're like most writers, you're a naturally lousy publicist when the subject is yourself. You write more handily about sudsing scum off the sides of a toilet bowl than extolling your virtues.

How do you overcome this? Pretend you're writing about a friend or imagine you're a top public relations writer assigned to promote a gifted client. Address yourself in the third person, using "she" in place of "I" and watch your unfounded modesty vanish. When you're finished, change the "she"s to "I"s.

Exactly what will you say to sway a sophisticated editor who's heard it all? You'll say things that no other writer in the world can say—except you. If you find this nearly impossible, think about what makes you special as a writer. What talents do you bring to the story?

OK, I'll go first. I've been told I have an ear for quotes and for picking just the right words to make a point or to cast a mood. I think

I'm good at exploiting the drama and I know I'm tenacious about trying to please an editor.

Now, I may not actually write this to an editor, but reflecting on it makes me feel better about myself. And when I write the bio, that added oomph of confidence comes through and helps me think about things I may actually say. OK. Your turn, I'm listening.

You may begin your bio by noting any major publications where you've published. If your words haven't hit the pages of *The New Yorker* yet, don't despair. Clips from regional and local publications count too, as long as they show fresh ideas and style.

When an editor from *Writer's Digest* magazine attended my seminar in Cleveland, one woman asked him if it were OK to send editors at national publications local clippings. His answer was perfect, "Send any clips you're proud of."

But in lieu of listing publications the editor's never heard of, emphasize the writing you've done. Say something like, *I've published a variety of articles in Mid-Atlantic publications including personality profiles, investigative pieces, first-person essays and 'as told to' stories.*

If your work inspired a rush of letters to the editor, say so. If an article resulted in a readers' response to clean up a neighborhood park, mention it. But skip that your mother phoned saying she always knew you were talented.

Next consider writing-related jobs—paid or volunteer. Have you done public relations work? Taught English? Written corporate communications? Did you edit a community newsletter? These are all pluses. There's no reason to explain that the Triple-E Caring Center Chronicle was a nonpaying position, though for sure with some editors passion counts more than pay.

How about college degrees? Undergraduate degrees probably mean little unless they're relevant to what you're writing or are from an Ivy League school. Graduate degrees carry more weight.

But never let your lack of formal education intimidate you. You don't need multiple letters after your name to be considered an expert. All editors really care about is what you write. If you or the woman you're profiling has launched a profitable business on a shoestring from home, editors will want to hear about it and they won't care if its creator has an M.B.A.

Drawing since you were nine? You may be a natural for writing a profile on the nationally renowned watercolor artist coming to town. Editors, and their readers, are impressed by those with life experiences.

Silence all those little voices telling you to be humble. No single characteristic turns an editor's head. What impresses and finally convinces her that you are the writer she wants for the story is adding one detail after another until you've drawn a portrait she can't resist.

What it all comes down to, one editor confided, is the e-word: enthusiasm. If she had to choose between two writers, one who was highly published but blasé about the story idea and a beginner with few credentials but a burning desire to write the story, guess which writer she'd choose.

You got it, the beginner. Why? Because the fire in your belly drives you to ask the one question that's so embarrassing it stuck to your mouth like peanut butter. But your reader wants to know, so you asked. This passion pushes you to nail down yet another detail or to follow a hunch to where an uninspired writer would never go. This Olympian zeal leads to inspiration, insights and unique views that capture a reader's imagination. It also sells publications, keeps editors successful and makes you happy.

Toward the end, put in a line offering to answer any questions and to follow up on any suggestions the editor may have. This is important because editors are sometimes hesitant to ask a writer to change the slant or focus of a story.

Seal the letter with your one-line vision of the story, something like, "'Reunited At Last' will inspire readers to pick up a pen, dial the phone or knock on a door and reconnect with the friend who once meant so much."

If you've worked with the editor before, you might add a personal comment such as how much you enjoyed a recent story that she worked on, or tell her something brief about your writing life. Or you can simply close with "Thank you."

Now after telling you all this, I'm going to add a disclaimer. Like all love letters, the best ones come from deep within yourself. They express your individuality. Nothing could be worse than a pile of letters arriving on an editor's desk all sounding like they were written by writers who read the same advice books—and, mindlessly, followed the rules to the letter. How could an editor expect a thoughtful, creative article from a writer whose query letter was an imitation?

I've given you guidelines, rules of sorts, that have worked for me and others. Help yourself to what you like, then add something that no one else can: yourself.

Weight Watchers

THE FIRST TIME AN EDITOR from a women's magazine asked for a photo of the woman I wanted to write about, "just to get an idea of what we're dealing with," I complied.

The next time I gagged.

"When a reader opens to an article, the first thing she looks at is the picture," the editor explained slightly embarrassed. "It's important the subject looks good."

"Looks good."

The words soured my sensibilities. Here was yet another filter for women to pass through. "Is she good looking?" These words trickle out of the mouth of editors who should know better. Editors from magazines claiming to empower women. What's "good-looking?" I wondered. Is there a standard? Do measurements count? How about the shape of her nose. Does breast size matter? Suppose they're not real?

Would we be asking the same of a man?

Writers know that magazines need to make money. They know that editors mirror the reader in articles, photos and advertisements. If a reader doesn't see herself between its covers, she doesn't buy it.

Writers also know that all women's magazines are not alike. Some seem slightly different while others appear to be from a different stratosphere. You clearly sense, for instance, that the younger, hipper women profiled in *Glamour*, *Mademoiselle* or *New Women* might not have a lot to say to their older, more conservative sisters spread across the pages of *Good Housekeeping*, *Family Circle* or *Woman's Day*. You can imagine the tight squeeze a woman featured in *Ladies' Home Journal* might experience if she tried to appear in the sassier, harder-edged *Redbook*.

Women featured in magazines must fit each magazine's reader skintight: age, socioeconomic status, attitude, sometimes even geography.

But that still doesn't dismiss a distressing phenomenon that seems to be spreading. Editors who have earned my respect—ones who return calls promptly, keep writers current on the status of their stories and say things like "great piece" and "thank you"—are now asking even more pointed questions about women's appearances, and without throat-clearing.

Not long ago a story of mine was killed when the editor saw the heroine's photo. This was a story so strong it inspired a CBS television movie starring Cybil Shepherd. But this editor of a mass circulation supermarket magazine groaned, "She's huge."

Granted, at five-foot four, 140 pounds, Joyce was not Vogue mate-rial, but she was the average American woman. She *was* the reader of this publication. This same magazine editor who thumbed her nose at Joyce's extra inches, chooses to drench her cover month after month with the same words: "diet, diet, diet."

"That's just the point," she countered. "Our readers *don't* want to read about someone who looks like them, they want to read about some-one who inspires them."

Now this is not to say that there's no place in magazines for the woman with the supposedly average American figure, quite the con-trary. The latest rage is the plus-size model, blond, blue-eyed, peachy complexion, 5-foot 10-inches, 155 pounds—and 25. But the point is that these women are set apart, labeled "queen size," and the editors who feature them on their pages seem a little too pleased with them-selves for appreciating their beauty.

Writing this makes me feel sleazy. You'd think we would have graduated by now from talking about women and weight. It should be a moot issue, but it's spoken louder than ever from pages where women are always youthful, slim, smart and economically advantaged. What this says to real women is that we're worth less than the box of bones my son was issued his first day of medical school.

Too many of us identify with the cartoon of a doctor diagnosing a middle age woman saying, "There's nothing wrong. You're feeling just like you should: angry, bitter and powerless."

Oddly enough, the very magazines that purport to raise women's self-esteem tend to diminish it by their editorial choices that seem sex-ist and ageist. I once wrote an article profiling three women. Two of them were in their 30s and the third was 50-something. The editor chose, sight unseen, to photograph only the two younger women. "For the third one, we'll get a picture of the cat," he said matter-of-factly.

Now if the woman is an oddity, then it's a different story. *USA Weekend*, with 40 million readers, featured on its cover the first woman three-star general in the army. *Fortune* published a long story, complete with photos, on a woman in her 60s running a multimillion dollar business.

This limited thinking trickles down to families too. Single parent families are accepted if the mom's hip, the dad's Wall Street-minted or a jock and the kids appear fresh out of The Gap.

When people are featured in a major magazine it's not unusual for the magazine's photo department to dress them for the shoot. They'll coordinate clothes, hair styles and makeup of everyone in the picture. Some women are pleased by the attention and relish what comes down to a total make-over. But a few consider it an intrusion. One woman swears her dog wouldn't stop growling at her for a week he was so confused by her new look. Another refused to be photographed in an outfit she didn't like. The editor moaned until the woman agreed to be draped in a scarf the photo department declared to be "her colors."

Some of this photography borders on genius. I've opened publications and barely recognized the woman I'd interviewed. The photographer had softened a smile, widened close-set eyes, bobbed a nose or worked some other magic.

Knowing this, I have to wonder why all the fuss? Next time I'm asked, "What does she look like? She's not heavy, is she?" I'll shoot back with, "How good is your photographer?"

Now, having said all this, like a chameleon I can cozy up to both camps. I truly understand any woman who resents being packaged, or worse, passed over by a publication. Yet I also empathize with editors. As writers we worry every word. But the reader may never get to those hard-earned words if the photo doesn't reach out to her and convey the right feeling.

I confess to mentioning in a query when a woman and her family are especially photogenic. I've even tucked in the envelope a photo from a newspaper or a snapshot. But I'm quick to stress how incredibly forthright, articulate and introspective she is. In other words, I make the point that her brain size is far more important than her bra size.

🐦 🐦 🐦

You may feel powerless to change what goes on in editorial havens in distant cities, but you can control what comes out of your computer. And occasionally, if you're like me, you, too, might need a tap on the wrist. Not long ago, a woman, whom I was profiling for *McCall's*, took me to school on writing about the disabled. I felt pretty sure of myself. I knew, for instance, not to say "Mary is a disabled woman," but instead to phrase it, "Mary is a woman who is disabled." A slight but important distinction. But I hadn't thought of the difference between labeling a woman "wheelchair bound," and "a wheelchair user." One implies helplessness, the other choice. I changed my manuscript to reflect my new enlightenment, but when the story was published "wheelchair bound" was back. I guess consideration sometimes takes a backseat to editorial inertia.

❧ As writers we worry every word. But the reader may never get to those hard-earned words if the photo doesn't reach out to her and convey the right feeling. I confess to mentioning in a query when a woman and her family are especially photogenic.

Here's an exercise to check for stereotypes in your writing. First describe an imaginary subject in three words, such as "blind, paralyzed, woman." Next, state three characteristics about her that wouldn't surprise anyone: "wheelchair-user, listens to books on tape, assisted by a guide dog." Then describe a characteristic that would startle your reader, something she wouldn't expect from this person. For instance, my subject, who is blind, commutes to work in a large city an hour away.

Do this with every woman whose story you write. Dig deep so you can reach beyond her blondness, her age, or her occupation, to capture her individuality.

Can We Talk?

WHEN YOU WANT TO TELL A WOMAN'S STORY you must get her permission. Imagine you are that woman. You've experienced a real-life drama that your small town newspaper featured in the middle of page two. Your friends phoned, your neighbors gossiped. Then, just as every copy of that paper except yours is relegated to the trash, you get a call from Ms. Freelance, whom you've never heard of, saying she wants to interview you. She says she's sure editors from *Mag World* would salivate to bring your tale to their millions of readers.

What do you say?

A few years back you might have dropped the baby and told her the coffee's on, come on over. But times have changed. Immediately you start seeing stars: Geraldo, Oprah or Jerry Springer. They lay stretch limos out at your feet and nights at hotels with Godiva chocolates on fluffed pillows in exchange for a few of your emotionally-wrought comments. You picture how young you'll look on TV.

Or instead of stars, you see dollars signs. You search your memory for the exact millions that other woman got for *her* story—a story you're sure was not half as good as yours. While getting such a deal is as likely as Ed McMahon appearing on your door step, those six-figure sums for personal ordeals stick like oatmeal to your memory.

And if fame or fortune doesn't sabotage the story, a severe attack of tabloid phobia may. Did she say *The Philadelphia Inquirer*, or simply *The Enquirer?* How can you be sure?

Today it takes more than chutzpah for a beginning freelance writer to get an interview. I know you probably don't want to hear this, but it takes all those things your teachers preached back in elementary school: planning, work, insight. And all you wanted was fun. Hold on, the fun's coming.

Consider this. You're asking a perfect stranger to bare her soul to you. You want to get inside her psyche and probe for truths she never knew existed. You're asking to become intimate—fast. If you do your job, you may end up knowing more about her than you do the partner with whom you share your bed. So first you must help her answer that all-important question: "What's in it for me?"

Here it helps to be a tad sneaky. You can't come shooting like John Wayne or she'll duck for cover. Instead you have to let her discover the benefits for herself—all in the first three minutes of your call.

To make this happen, do your homework. You're wasting your time if you pick up the phone, purse your lips and purr like the twenty-something women on AT&T television commercials, with little regard for your subject's wants and needs. At this point it's more important what's in her head than what's in yours. So your first job is to find out.

Play sleuth. Learn all you can about her before you call. Dissect the news clipping, the television blurb or whatever led you to the story idea. Somewhere there will be a hint as to what motivates this woman, what gets her out of bed each morning, besides a mortgage or crying kids. Sometimes you have to go further in this discovery phase. You might speak with others that know her or, if she's been in the news before, check out what's been written about her at the library or on the internet. The clues are there, it's your job to put the pieces together.

Many years ago an editor at *Family Circle* asked me to come up with a proposal about a preservationist whom she could feature in her "Women Who Make A Difference" column. Immediately my mind flashed to St. Clair Wright, the virtual savior of Maryland's historic capital, Annapolis. In the 1950s, St. Clair put her body between the wrecking balls of overzealous developers and the venerable buildings. As I dialed this septuagenarian's number, my mind raced through my week. Where would I fit her in? My thoughts should have been elsewhere. St. Clair was not impressed with being profiled in *Family Circle* or anywhere. She'd had her share of accolades and didn't want to rehash the battles she fought long ago with the community leaders.

If I had done my homework, I would have known that she was fighting a new battle: terminal cancer. More important, I would have sensed that what really mattered to her was the cause to which she devoted her life: historic preservation. Luckily, a member of the local preservation group pointed out to Mrs. Wright that this was an opportunity to make historic preservation a household term. *Family Circle*, a supermarket tabloid with the largest readership of any woman's publication in the world, would bring this typically highbrow cause into the kitchens of middle-class America. St. Clair agreed and became one of the most enthusiastic participants I've ever worked with on a story.

Some women wear their cause like a cape, boldly swung over their shoulder for all to see. Typical of these women are those who have suffered life's tragedies. Their missions are transparent.

Sometimes the woman's concern about her special cause is shrouded by the hubbub of life, but her feelings about it are often near the surface and a little polite, gentle searching may reveal them. It is when we tap into these feelings that we uncover a powerful tool for gaining consent to write our story. When you ask a woman "can we talk?" be sure the cause that's close to her heart is close to yours.

Sandy Barnes, a Wisconsin state trooper, donated the liver of her young son, killed on a bike, to save the life of 20-year-old Maria. In turn, Maria named her first child after Sandy's son and asked Sandy to be his godmother.

Sandy willingly relived the tragic details with me for a *Family Circle* drama because she wanted readers everywhere to know her child and to know the difference organ donations can make.

Others open their financial books to readers because they want to validate their lives. When I wrote "Don't Pay for it—Trade for it!" for *Family Circle's* money column, I featured three women who made their dreams come true without ever opening a wallet: One traded purebred puppies for her newborn's obstetrician's fee, another put her daughter through private school by exchanging her homemade egg rolls for tuition and a third refurbished an old Victorian home by bartering jewelry she found at garage sales for goods and services.

🐛 🐛 🐛

Sometimes you're stymied by the sheer logistics of reaching a woman with a great story. How do you contact someone with a un-listed phone number? Here's another place your feminine wiles come in. Usually somewhere, in even the tiniest clip, blurb or announcement, is some indication of a job, a group or other link this person shares with the community. Read carefully and you'll usually find it. Or try working through an organization's public relations office. These professionals are paid to get their people in print, they'll be happy to help. But beware. They may swamp you with material, not all of which is appropriate. Use them as a springboard to relevant information.

If the story is hot and your subject's avoiding the press, be creative. One writer wanting to reach a mother of quintuplets sent flowers to her hospital room with a note asking if they might speak. The woman phoned to thank the writer and the assignment was clinched.

Never be intimidated. Sometimes the busiest people are the most accessible. My husband, Allen, swears that if he needs a doctor fast he's going to pose as a writer. Doctors are suckers for publicity. Now mind you, I'm not trashing doctors, remember my middle son's studying to become one. But these harried professionals make themselves amazingly available to writers. One took my call en route to surgery. He was already scrubbed so a nurse propped the receiver up to his ear.

Now once your subject says hello, work smart. You'll want to name drop any mutual acquaintances, then quickly tell her who you are. You've got 10 seconds to endear yourself to her. Try something like, "I'm Susan Murphy, a freelance writer from Greensville, and I was so moved when I read your story in the local paper that I'd like to propose it to the editors of..." Don't worry if you haven't been published yet— but don't mention it. Instead let your enthusiasm for the story spill out. Avoid weasel expressions like "Maybe an editor might be interested." Sound confident, because if you don't, another writer will, and guess who will win the interview.

It's a mistake to mention the word "contract" because, understandably, some women will think it translates to big money. They see $20,000 while you, if you're lucky, will see a few thousand.

Be careful, also, not to make writing the story sound too wonderful—and easy. One time my enthusiasm backfired. While scouring for a true life drama for *Reader's Digest*, I learned of an attorney from Maryland who, along with her boyfriend, was rescued from the rim of a volcano in Ecuador. Before she returned home, I'd charmed her mother into interceding for me with her daughter.

Once she arrived in the states I waited for her to catch her breath, then I phoned. She greeted me warmly, listening intently to my description of the process. First, we'd speak for a half hour or so on the phone. Next I'd write a proposal, then after I got the go-ahead to write the story, we'd speak in depth, reliving it, moment-by-moment. It will be sensual. It will be dramatic. It will be great. Her friends will be impressed, I told her. I was so good, she believed every last word. So much so that she decided right there on the spot she was going to keep all that fun for herself.

"C'mon," I snickered to myself. "Lawyers make lousy writers. This is my passion and you're going to whip it out, just like that and for the *Digest* no less."

Did I say it out loud? Of course not. I knew then and there we'd reached the point of no return. Did she ever write it? Not a chance.

So when you set the literary scene for your subject, strike a balance. It'll be a great experience, you imply, but only because you, a competent writer, will be handling it. Offer to follow-up your call with a letter, to send copies of any pieces you've published. Offer to meet with her.

Explain early on how much time you'll need. You can safely err on the short side, because once she begins telling her story the odds are she'll enjoy it. Be sure to ask if she has any questions. It helps to overcome hesitations, to clear the way for those eyeball-to-eyeball talks.

In three golden minutes you convince her to trust you with her story. Then you ask her for what's known as the exclusive. Before the proliferation of talk shows and people-driven magazines it was safe to say that a story found in a small town newspaper was yours. But this is no longer a done deal. Once a wire service picks up a piece, it can evoke a media feeding frenzy. This is why you must make her understand how important it is that she speak to no other writers doing magazine or national newspaper features—until your story is published. (Most editors of larger publications don't care if a story has appeared in a small or local publication.)

I never used to ask for this. What right did I have? I never paid for a story. Some editors would look askance at money passing between the woman and the writer—I do thank her with a small gift and clippings of the article. But I've learned that publishing has changed. You must clearly get the exclusive up front.

Let me tell you what can happen if you don't. After working two months on a story for *Family Circle*, the editor killed it when another writer's version appeared in the "Style" section of the Sunday *Washington Post*. I'd spent hours with the subject and she, too, was disappointed to learn her story wouldn't run in her favorite magazine.

Last summer another *Family Circle* story was killed when the woman reneged on our agreement to keep the story fresh until it appeared on the newsstand. This mother was reunited with a daughter she had given up for adoption 33 years earlier. The Caucasian mother had become pregnant with when she was raped by an African-American man. The daughter had also sought out her mother, accompanied by an entertainment lawyer who handled magazine, book and movie rights. Soon after I'd been granted, in writing, the exclusive magazine rights, the lawyer phoned asking if the mother and daughter could appear on the "Today Show" on the Fourth of July. I screamed no and he acquiesced. But then I was infomed that the mother, daughter, her husband and their five children chose to reunite again in Boston's Durgen

Park—complete with hugs and tears—five weeks after their first emotional encounter there. (Guess they liked the place.) This second time they were greeted by a slew of siblings, aunts, uncles, cousins—and an even larger gathering of photographers and reporters who "just happened to hear of the reunion."

The *Family Circle* photographer assigned to the story could barely make it through the crowd. Naturally, when the editor learned what happened, she wanted no part of an also-ran story and instantly killed it.

What did I do wrong? Nothing. Sometimes telling women's stories stinks. Luckily, it's not often.

Be proud of what you're offering. You're giving your subject a little bit of fame, acceptance and the opportunity to explain her world. You're the shrink without the bill. And in return, you're asking for her loyalty. I'd say it's a fair deal, and if you think it is, so will she.

You Don't Say

LET'S PRETEND YOU'RE ONE OF 25 STUDENTS in my writing workshop. Only hours before we've all exchanged names, serial numbers and other pleasantries. Now, as we all sit in a circle, I ask each of you to think hard, really hard, of the worst, most despicable thing you've ever done in your entire life. Something so low, your dog would abandon you if he ever found out. The room falls quiet. Then I say that after you've decided what it is, you're going to take turns and, one at a time, you're going to reveal this seamy side of yourself. You look at me, you look at the exit. You calculate the steps.

OK. Take a minute or two to think.

Need more time? No rush, we'll wait.

Ready?

Now tell us what you have really been doing since I asked you to divulge your darkest secret.

Were you honestly reviewing the moments of your life for those times when you grew fur, sprouted fangs and foamed at the mouth? Or were you scrambling to come up with something else, something a bit naughty that will get me off your back, but not provoke the others to corner you in the parking lot on your way home. At the very least, you looked for something to save face.

This is exactly what happens when you arrive at your subject's home, plop down in the chair, take out the pad, turn on the recorder and ask her the first question. She wants beauty and you want truth.

Being a woman, she also wants a friend. She wants someone who will empathize with her struggles, find form in the crazy quilt of her days and make sense out of how she's spending her life. In a word, she wants someone she can trust. And all you want is a story.

So what's a writer to do? Can you be her confidant and Barbara Walters at the same time? You've got no choice. Interviewing's not Burger King: You cannot have it your way.

Think of an interview as a birth. You, the writer, are the midwife delivering meaning for seemingly random events.

Gary Sledge, a director of *Reader's Digest*, puts it this way, "Beginning writers look for someone to give them the story, but the story is formed on the interviewer's ear."

Plan ahead. Not knowing what you want out of an interview is as bad as going to Filene's Basement with nothing in mind. Sure you might uncover a designer original in the bottom of the heap, but more likely you'll cart home clothes that are candidates for next April's garage sale.

Magically, or maybe not so magically, when you know where you're headed with a story, the quotes, anecdotes and insights gleaned from the interview tend to flow in support of your take, your angle, your point of view. Not the other way around.

Begin long before you ask your first question. As soon as you decide to write the story, step into the woman's life to figure out what you want out of it. There are many ways to subconsciously assume her identity.

Start by reading anything written about her or by her—even her sixth grade journal or high school diary if you can get your hands on it. Talk, better yet, listen to anyone and everyone who knows her including friends, family, neighbors, even enemies. Especially enemies.

Then interview yourself. Ask yourself why this woman's story intrigued you. What are you curious about? What questions do you want answered? Nothing's off limits. Be sure to include a few bold, embarrassing ones.

Next, think deeply about the story. With only the foundation of facts you have at this point, how do you envision your story? What two or three questions seem pivotal to the piece? The answers to these few questions are the information you cannot leave the interview without. Commit these to memory. Write them on your forearm.

Slowly you'll notice a portrait developing, a direction to plot your course.

One caveat: If, as you interview, research and ponder, you discover that your original take was skewed, tweak your take to make it fit the new improved version. Once in a while you might find your mind was as overcharged as your credit card when you concocted your original take. When this happens, pitch the original take and start again.

This focus is important, think of the alternative: With no point in mind, you research and interview randomly, coming up with everything, which is nothing. You have neither the time nor the energy to do this, let alone the space to write it. And your reader won't sit for it. She wants your thumbprint on a feature article. She doesn't want to know everything about this woman, just the one aspect you thought worth mentioning.

This is a good time, if you have an assignment or an interested editor, to nail down who the reader is and any special angle the editor wants. Editors appreciate this. I heard one say she can always clean up the copy of a poor writer, but she can't fill in the holes of a poor interviewer. If you're interviewing to flesh out a query, decide to which publications you'll pitch the idea and interview with the readers of those publications in mind.

Before the interview, pull out a book on body language. You're not going to give Freudian interpretations to your subject's every tic, but you might want to note a revealing gesture, a telling side glance, a twiddle of a stray hair, one hand to her head or her heart, then let your reader take it from there.

A few days before your interview, give your subject a casual "just want to check the time" type call. Then mention the angle you think the story will take. Mind you, you're not asking her permission or even seeking her opinion. You're sharing the underpinnings of the piece, the girders that support it, so ideas, insights and opinions can percolate in her subconscious. And, by the time the two of you talk, full-bodied thoughts will spew out of her lips. You're making her a partner in the piece, painlessly. Of course, you don't tell her any of this. She just thinks you're warm and sharing.

Never, never ask the zingers until the right time in the interview. Without your hand holding, it may turn her off. Even if it doesn't, you don't want her to open a vein too early.

Now to the meeting itself. Try to create a faux social situation in which your subject will relax and reveal.

Unless she has kids rowdy enough convince you to double-up on your birth control, ask to meet her at home. Her turf will give you clues about what's important to her. Check it out.

You notice her son's hockey picture. Your son played hockey too. You commiserate about ice time at 2 a.m., the freezing rinks, the crazy mothers who sewed umpire dolls then tore them apart limb by limb if they didn't like a call. Now you've established a common bond. A bond that will make you both more relaxed.

Sometimes the clues a home yields can save the story. When Joanna Powell, entertainment editor for *Good Housekeeping*, interviewed Martha Stewart at the East Hampton beach house, Martha had a new cookbook coming out and she wouldn't stray from pitching her recipes. So instead, the writer detoured. As Martha ruminated on such things as the virtues of raising chickens for fresh eggs, Joanna scanned the room. She noticed Martha's fetish for antique taxidermy. Everywhere there were stuffed fish, some huge. In the study, under glass, were giant insects from Africa. And in the powder room above the toilet was a smiling blow fish. Against this backdrop, the story survived.

If your subject shies away from bringing you home, ask if you can work out with her at the gym, or accompany her when she picks up her child at day care. See her in action. But be sure to include some quiet time too, when you both can get away to talk.

Worst places: sitting across her desk or in a noisy restaurant. If she insists on dining out, forget crab feasts or ribs and choose something you could eat in your sleep. Remember the focus is on her, not on the food.

If your story hinges on your subject baring her soul to you, you might want to consider a "let's get to know each other" meeting first. When I interviewed the mother of Christa McAuliffe for "The Whole World Loved My Daughter," the story commemorating the tenth anniversary of the Challenger space shuttle explosion, I knew that for the story to work I had to earn Grace Corrigan's trust.

One of the ways to earn trust is to spend time with your subject. Let me digress a bit. When I travel on assignment, I always stay in hotels. Yes, the publication picks up the tab, but even if it didn't, after interviewing for hours, the solitude a hotel room provides, to gather your thoughts, review your notes, decide what you've got and what you still need, is worth every dollar. But once I broke my rule. And I'm glad I did. Here's what happened.

When I phoned Grace Corrigan to plan my trip to her home outside Boston, she invited me to stay with her. I thanked her, but declined. She assured me it was no trouble adding, "But it's only a small room. If it's not good enough, I understand." Mrs. Corrigan, now a widow living in a three bedroom ranch-style home in the suburbs, really wanted me to stay. How could I refuse?

I arrived in Boston late afternoon and took a cab from Boston's Logan airport to her home. Our plan was to start work early the next day, breaking only for a quick tour of the Challenger Learning Center at nearby Framingham State College and continue until evening. So that night we went to her favorite restaurant for dinner. (Yes, *McCall's* paid for it.)

Over New England clam chowder, lobster and a glass of wine, we talked as women and as mothers. I told her I had admired Christa's spunk and how much I had laughed reading how it took to the end of first period class for Christa's curls to dry. I told Grace that I, too, have been known to arrive at appointments with soggy locks. We talked about Grace's other children, her grandchildren and her husband who lost his battle to cancer five years after Christa's death.

She honored my one rule: We would not talk about Christa until the next day. This was a chance to get to know one another. Although she was playing on home court, I'd come with the advantage. I already knew something about Grace Corrigan but to her I was only a voice on the phone. I needed to show her I cared deeply about her story and wanted it to reflect what she's felt since that cold day when America stared at their television sets in disbelief at the ghoulish image of the exploding shuttle. If she was going to let me probe the depths of her heart, she'd have to trust me.

Although that evening we spoke of everyone but Christa, I came away feeling that my hunch on this seventy-something woman was dead wrong. This was not going to be a major Kleenex interview. Grace's story would not be sappy or sentimental. It would have a tone of its own. She was, indeed, very proud of her daughter's life. But she was also very accepting of her death. She had found peace, and her words conveyed it: "Christa died at one of the happiest moments of her life with people she greatly admired. We should all be so lucky."

Over the Corrigan living room fireplace hangs the official NASA portrait of Christa in her sky-blue flight suit, smiling broadly. Lining the entire hallway are photos of Christa: Christa receiving first communion; Christa pledging Girl Scouts; Christa marrying Steve; Christa hugging daughter, Caroline and son, Scott. In the study framed letters from world leaders share space with letters from school children.

But the sentiment that struck me the most was one from Christa herself, stuck on the refrigerator door. The card, yellowing with age, read: "Behind every great woman is another woman. Thanks, Mom. Christa"

As I fell asleep that night in the twin maple bed, I noticed a model of the Challenger shuttle on the dresser. Its image, cast against the wall by the glow of a street lamp outside the window, rose across the ceiling as if reaching for heaven.

And to think I nearly stayed in a hotel.

🐭   🐭   🐭

When you settle down to interview, take out your notebook and recorder and then forget the recorder is there (well, almost). Focus all your energies on two things: making your subject feel comfortable and active listening. You'll want to remember everything your mother told you to do the first time you met your Aunt Tilda. You can skip the curtsy but nothing else: make eye contact, smile, acknowledge what your subject is saying and show you appreciate her sharing. Even if you're getting nothing, fake it, you might eventually get something. Acting bored, disinterested or hostile will get you nothing but the door.

It's not a bad idea early on to be a bit confessional yourself, to reveal a wart or two, so to speak. A modelesque young woman who heads a large New England communications firm confided to me after my workshop how she put her subjects at ease. "No matter how hard I tried to be friendly, I intimidated some women," she says. "Then one day I forgot to latch my purse and in the middle of an interview it dropped and makeup, pens, pads, coupons (yes! coupons), even a tampon rolled across the floor. Suddenly the two of us are down on our knees rushing to gather the junk—and laughing." Since then, I've "forgotten" several times to latch my purse when interviewing. Another ploy is to ask for a glass of water. She says, "The simple act of handing me something I need helps give my subject the upper hand."

Now you may think you'd never cause anyone's knees to shake, but never forget the power of your pen. To your subject you are *New Woman*, *Allure* or *The Los Angeles Times*.

Set a warm, approachable tone in the first five minutes of the interview. Remember the movie *Speechless* when Michael Keaton, a speech writer for one senatorial candidate, tells Gena Davis, a writer for the opposition, why the public's serving her candidate to the sharks. "You must show the voters that your man has heart, offers hope and that he gets warm," Keaton says. You must show your subject that you, too, have heart, offer hope and get warm.

Like most things, empathy is best conveyed in specifics. While, by the grace of God, I've never endured the pain of losing a child, when I interviewed Sandy Barnes, who had lost two, I confided the grief I'd felt when our son Scott suffered the eye injury.

This wasn't a ploy. It was sharing, woman to woman. While I was quick to distinguish between my son's loss of sight and her son's loss of life, as mothers we shared experiences that years later still make us sick to our stomachs when we wake in the middle of the night.

Good interviewing begins with an understanding of what it all means. Ted Gup, a former *Washington Post* reporter and a Hopkins writing teacher, said it best: "What your subject fears most in an interview is a loss of control. She's afraid you're going to misinterpret something and she's going to be crucified by readers. Put your subject at ease. Give her control. Tell her that anytime she doesn't want to talk about something, to just say so. Now here's the good part: Once she knows she has this power, she exhales. And she seldom, very, very seldom, uses it."

Once your subject begins speaking, listen—really listen. Remember poet A. E. Housman's words: "Don't understand me too quickly." Let her picture develop slowly, steadily. Strive to hear beyond her words. How does she speak? Loudly? In a whisper? Does she hesitate? Is she emphatic? Does she look you in the eye?

Engage your right brain, intuit, tune into your feelings and mark these feelings in your notebook. They may be the most meaningful part of the interview.

As you listen, piece the new information within the picture you already have. Does it fit? If not, why? Ask yourself, What is she *not* saying?

Continue stroking by speaking her language. It's not by chance that a savvy car salesman falls into step with you as he leads you to the new models on the lot. You want to speak like her, so she doesn't start speaking like you. There are few things worse than reading quotes in a feature article that sound like they came from the writer's mouth, not the subject's.

Speak in the tone you plan for the article. Why talk with the cadence of a funeral dirge if you want to write a side-slapping comedic piece. Matching your tone to the article's will help generate more usable information.

Nonfiction writing guru Gay Talese recommends parroting, repeating the subject's last three or four words as a question. Bestselling author Stephen Covey takes it a step further, suggesting that the empathetic listener rephrase the content of the speaker's words and reflect her feeling.

She: "Before my husband told me he was leaving me, all the signs were there."

You: "All the signs were there, you sensed something wasn't right?"

She: "Yes, he worked late every night. Forgot my birthday, never noticed if I changed my hairstyle."

You: " You felt hurt, so you tried getting his attention by changing your hair?"

She: "I made myself over. I tried becoming another person, a person he might want."

This method encourages your subject to go deeper, to probe herself, to give you a more refined quote. She's actually editing herself.

Two magic words to remember: when and why. Both elicit specifics.

She says, "It was the toughest time of my life."

You ask, "When?"

She says, "When my son told me he wanted to find his biological mother."

You ask, "Why?"

"Because he said that now that he knew the truth he could never feel the same about me."

Let's try another.

She says, "I made sure my daughter had an education, even if I had to work three jobs."

"Why?"

"Because we're descendants of slaves and it wasn't slavery that I feared but ignorance. I promised myself when she was born that she would go to college."

If your subject's tongue is wrapped around her esophagus, try loosening her up by taking a leap. Say something like, "I'll bet when your husband's eighth wife appeared on your doorstep you..." Fill in the blank. It isn't important if she agrees with your conjecture. What matters is that she begins thinking along those lines.

You know what else it does, it compliments her by showing her that you're really listening. This kind technique works well with friends too.

If the sounds of silence make you uneasy, count to 10, slowly, very slowly. Refrain from filling the pauses, let your subject do it after she's had the time to gather her thoughts, mull over her emotions.

Some editors, like those at *Reader's Digest,* suggest letting the subject just speak her mind, because if she talks long enough she's bound to say something worth writing. That's fine if you're on the *Digest's* generous tab and if she's willing to let you move in with her. To me, this sounds too happenstance. I choose to be surprised by serendipity, not dependent upon it.

Be patient and caring, but feel free to press your subject, always keeping your goal in mind. Sometimes in an effort to charm our subject, we're charmed right back and we forget the very reason we're there.

Identify and push her hot buttons. Spot these by noticing how she answers a question or where she takes a topic. Pay attention to your intuition to know when you're getting close to the jugular. And when you are, be relentless, but subtle.

It's better to create an atmosphere that spurs revelations rather than extracting them one-by-one like impacted wisdom teeth. When you achieve this, she'll put down her defenses and give you quotes that burn through the page.

Now, remember those two or three questions you jotted on your forearm—the ones you decided were critical to your story? Take a peak at those pivotal questions before you say good-bye to be sure you've gotten your answers.

🍒 🍒 🍒

Sometimes you'll need experts' opinions, doctors, lawyers, engineers, to shore up your women's stories. And often these professionals speak like they've been locked up with a computer too long. They often thrive on jargon and your job becomes translator, helping them speak the language of the reader. You must decipher the bloated, meaningless banter into real, generic, no-bull language. A good way is to ask, "Is this what you mean?" Then say it, aiming for one syllable words.

If your expert relishes jargon, she'll fight you word-for-word, insisting your interpretation is inaccurate. Yes, she'll even use that word, inaccurate—instead of wrong. But hold strong. Let her know this is horse manure and your readers are too smart to swallow it. Of course you don't say this, you smile and repeat your interpretation changing a word or phrase, but keeping the language real. If she's a genuine bull artist she may hang on for another go-round. Nothing worries these types more than having you take down the language, making them appear, in their view, less than incredibly intelligent to their colleagues. So dig in your claws. (Acrylic nails come in handy.)

Don't be afraid to frame a question:

"Would you agree that...?"

"Could we say that...?"

In rare cases you might have to soften your subject by telling her that her message is vital, and readers, being the fools we are, will never fully appreciate her wisdom unless it's presented in a way we dimwits can understand.

Notes on Quotes

"TELL ME EXACTLY WHAT SHE SAID, PLEAEEEEZE," you ask your friend. "And don't leave out a word."

Sound familiar? There's something about the precise words a woman chooses that gives your article power. When you write those words—words that come out of her mind, not yours—she comes alive on the page. If you're fussy about which words to quote, she comes across sounding like no one else in the world—now she's not only an individual, she's a woman with a passion for justice and a fetish for bald men who lisp.

No wonder when we interview, and later when we write, we become junkies for quotes that resonate from the speaker to the reader.

You know what else quotes do—even bad ones, but you won't write these—they open up the page. See for yourself. Look at lines of gray type. Now pretend you're a reader who has just put in eight hours on the job, you've driven an hour through traffic to get home, cleaned up after a puppy that believes newspaper should remain spotless, spoken with your son's teacher who said he's the impetus for her early retirement, fought with your husband over whether his mother can spend the weekend and then, and only then, you pick up a magazine.

Keep in mind that reading this may be the first thing you don't have to do today. And you do have choices. Your can watch a news magazine show, chat with a friend on the phone or just listen to the dishwasher churn. Will the appearance of a solid block of type win out over Stone Phillips' smile? Now picture that page broken up by a quote or two. Presto. It's got a chance. Your eyes slide down the page to the words boxed by those funny little marks and that reader-friendly white space. And before you give Stone's smile a second thought, you've landed at the bottom of the page.

No question about it. Quotes are a good thing. The problem is you, the writer, can't dial toll free and order a dozen. You've got to cultivate them, as tenderly as a new bud popping through a crusty New Hampshire spring snow.

Yet, as soon as you take out your notebook, prop your recorder and put up your imaginary antennae that beckons, "Wanted: raw emotion, honesty; bull need not apply," your subject raises her guard to keep from spewing what she really thinks and feels.

But if, as we discussed before, you focus on making her feel secure, appreciated and in control—and maybe if you're just a little lucky—unforgettable, quotable words will slip through her censor, spilling into your notebook.

One way to cultivate great quotes from a subject is to regale *her* with a great quote. Repeat the riveting words another woman used to describe a similar situation. Because your subject wants to please you, her subconscious will take over and start breeding her own.

The same goes for gathering compelling anecdotes, those little stories within the big story. It's human nature to want to top a joke or a story. Tell me a great one and I'll try to reciprocate. Do the same with your subject.

And when these wonderful quotes do come, you'll be grateful you didn't fall for the temptation to concoct your own. Readers have a built-in sensor that screams "fraud" when they read a made-up quote.

Besides lending reality to your story, a great quote provides insight. It gives the why behind the what. Great quotes often expose a person's motivation, like what—besides a paycheck—makes a woman get up every morning before dawn, gulp black coffee, then drive off in the lingering dark to a job in the next city.

Here are a few examples of quotes that say more than meets the page.

Penny Sass of Cherry Hill, New Jersey, believed that all children, no matter what their handicaps, should have a chance to play ball. The next two paragraphs from "Field of Dreams," published in *Family Circle*, show what truly motivated her to start her own special baseball team.

> Penny's dream of establishing a Challenger division in Cherry Hill began on the baseball field. Unlike other mothers who cheered when their sons hit a home run, Penny got a lump in her throat. As her older son, Michael, then 11, circled the bases, her 9-year-old son, Joey, who is neurologically impaired would ask "Can I play too?"
>
> One spring day in 1989 Penny decided she'd had enough. "That's it, I told myself. I'm going to do something. Joey is going to play baseball."

Consider what the quotes reveal in the lead of another *Family Circle* piece, "Reunited."

> On a summer afternoon in 1969, 6-year-old Melease McClain was rummaging through her grandmother's cedar chest when she spotted a birth certificate embossed with a gold seal. Intrigued, the first grader began sounding out the words on the parchment: Vicky Irene McClain.
>
> "Who is this?" Melease asked, running to her mother. Holding her daughter tightly, Barbara McClain, then 21, began to cry. "She's your little sister," she said. "She was taken from us long ago, but she'll be home someday."
>
> Melease told her mother not to cry anymore—"because I'm going to help you find her," she promised.

Take a look at a paragraph from *Family Circle*'s "The Greatest Gift of All," the story of Sandy Barnes, the mother who donated her dead child's liver to a young woman, saving her life.

> Her thoughts drifted back to one afternoon a year earlier, as she was signing the organ donor release statement on her new driver's license. When she told Richie what she was doing, he mumbled, "How gross."
>
> But she explained that if she weren't alive anymore and someone needed her organs in order to live, it would be a waste for *both* people to die. He agreed. Then he asked, "When I get my license, will you witness it so I can be an organ donor?"
>
> Now Sandy would honor her son's wish. She told a nurse that if he died, she'd like to donate his organs. "It was the only way to add a note of dignity to a senseless tragedy," she said.

"A Friend in Need," a *Family Circle* story, portrayed the extraordinary relationship between career woman, Janet Dodson and her "little sister" Mary Ta. As a Big Sisters of America volunteer, Janet nurtured Mary from an abused child of 10 to a law school student. Janet's devotion went beyond the usual Saturday morning relationship of most Big and Little Sisters. When Mary's home life erupted into violence, Janet took her under her roof, taking responsibility for the adolescent.

Why? the reader asks, and Janet answers in a quote:

> "I wanted more love in my life and I knew that in order to get it, I had to give it."

What do you notice about these quotes? Short. Short. Short. A few times editors have sent me the galley copy of a story ready to print and I've been surprised to see the revealing but longish quotes that I tenderly cultivated from a bare spark in the subject's eye pared to one or two lean sentences.

One editor even gave this paring a percentage: 37 percent culled. "How could she?" I pouted. Slashing a poignant quote seemed almost as painful as parting with a cat. But when my emotion cooled and I read the piece again—with the quotes pared—I liked it. Actually, I liked it a lot. Being succinct gave it punch.

Try doing this before you send your story to the editor. When you think you're finished editing the piece, but just before you send it in, aim to trim your quotes by at least one-third. If a quote is five sentences, for instance, try to prune it to two or three.

But what if the reader needs those deleted sentences to understand the gist of the piece? Paraphrase them. The point is, less is more.

Of course this is one of those rules that is just standing there, hands on hips, tongue out, taunting "nah-nah-nah-nah-nah." Find the exception. Find those wonderful paragraphs of spoken words that no editor would dare touch with a delete key, and include them, but be sure you're right.

Most of the time, the rules win out. When thinking quotes, think Katie Couric—short and punchy.

Your next job is to set the quotes up. Here's a drill I use with the students in my seminars. Take the quote,

> "It's raining today in Chicago," says Mary.

"Now what does that say?" I ask. They stare at me blankly like "Did we really pay all that money for this?"

"Nothing," I answer quickly. "But suppose we set up that quote with a little perspective?"

> After 21 days of torrential downpour, Mary looks out her window at the Chicago skyline and says, "It's raining today."

See how a shot of perspective or background elevates the meaning of the quote? After you've written your story, go back and scaffold your quotes with a sentence or two that makes them more potent. Even better, I tell my students, make those setup sentences a bit judgmental. They like this. They nod.

And when you write those quotes, have no qualms about merging a thought she said here with another she said there. Same goes for cleaning up the "ah-huhs, ummmms" and other verbal tics. In fact, any gentle reshaping that will help her make her point's OK.

> 🐭 *And when you write those quotes, have no qualms about merging a thought she said here with another she said there.*

Sometimes you come across some great material cloaked in awkward, rambling quotes. Paraphrase these quotes in a concise, elegant statement, then attribute those wonderful words to her—she'll love you for it—but don't enclose them in quotation marks.

Here's the one Golden Rule about quotes: Keep the tone and intent as spoken, and be sure she doesn't end up sounding like you.

Now one small point. Anytime you want to attribute a quote to a speaker, remember a four letter word: "said." A reporter I knew a long time ago never learned that word. Her speakers never said anything. They opined, exchanged verbal fisticuffs, threw barbs, raged, accused, argued, countered, insinuated. And, amazingly, they never did the same thing twice. If she's still writing, I'd hate to be her thesaurus.

Those high-test verbs are fine for charging up a dramatic moment, but rev them up too often and the reader shouts back "Whoa." Use "said," instead. It's a magic word that, even when used repeatedly, disappears when read.

🐭 🐭 🐭

Where, in the story or article, do you put quotes? Quotes are Hershey's kisses. Drop a few throughout to reward the reader for staying with you through the boring but important parts.

Some of us like to kick off a feature with a quote. But think about it. Unless those lines are really riveting, do you care what someone's saying when you haven't been introduced to the person who's saying it? The *Wall Street Journal* usually places its "wow" quote high in the feature article—but after the lead. The reader hears a human voice soon, but not so soon that she doesn't care what it's saying.

Hoard the winningest quote, though, for the closing. I've been schooled on this point by editors who have moved an especially poignant quote from the top of my story all the way down to the bottom.

"Suppose the reader goes into labor before she gets a chance to read the whole story," I'd protest, my writer's insecurity speaking.

"Forget it," editors insist. "Pulling that quote down to the end nails your message in the reader's mind."

Here are parting quotes that closed stories we talked about earlier.

"Field of Dreams":

> Pat insists that she is the real beneficiary. "I started out looking for a way for my son to play ball and I ended up with the greatest accomplishment of my life."

"A Friend in Need":

> "Before I met Janet, I wished I could end my own life. I know there will be challenges ahead. But I have a special place in my heart that tells me I can rise above them. I thank Janet for that place."

"The Greatest Gift of All":

> Running to greet "Grandma Sandy" on a recent visit, Ricky, now 2, gives her a big hug. Seeing the love between them, Maria says something she never forgets: "If it weren't for Richie and you, I wouldn't be here and neither would my boys. I can never thank you enough."
>
> "You already have," Sandy says warmly, as she cradles Isaac in her arms.

It doesn't matter if the quote leaves her singing, sobbing or swearing, as long as she's feeling.

The Drama

Life Through the Lens

ONE OF THE GREAT MYSTERIES, right up there with life after life and how O.J. walked, is why writers and photographers working on the same story seldom meet. Only once did I share visions with a photographer assigned to the same piece, and when it happened I thought—eureka!—this is the way it should always be!

What usually occurs is the writer does her job and then the photographer, given a thumbnail sketch of the story, snaps an image. Last year I traveled to West Virginia on assignment for *McCall's* to report on a mother and daughter who delivered babies four hours apart at the same hospital. The story was a play on the movie *Father of the Bride, Part 2.*

After two days of interviewing, I was waiting for the cab to take me to the airport when the photographer arrived. The jean-clad, bearded young man saddled with twin ebony leather camera bags barely nodded although I nearly jumped into his arms. I wanted to postpone my flight. I wanted to shadow him. I wanted to curl up in a corner and watch ever so closely his every move. I suspected that there was something to be learned from him and maybe, though I wasn't as certain of this, I could teach him a thing or two.

I wondered how he would position mother and daughter for a picture. Who would he put in the background? Who would be prominent? Would he vote with his lens to give the 21-year-old daughter greater importance than her 43-year-old mother? Would he capture them looking at one another or away, symbolic of their lives branching out? How would he handle the babies? Would the older mother glance lovingly at her own baby or her new granddaughter? Where would their husbands figure in this visual constellation?

Unable to shroud my delight, I bombarded him with questions. He mumbled a few words and continued to clean his lens. The next thing I knew, he was off to check if a neighboring home offered a more suitable backdrop. What was wrong with the daughter's modest home? I wondered. Was it lack of lighting or something less speakable? Hmmm.

This experience contrasted sharply with one a few months later. *Life* magazine assigned me to write about Janice DeBlois, a Massachusetts mother who reared a blind, autistic son to become a musical savant. Tony, who was about to graduate from Berklee College of Music, could not read or write. Indeed, he could not even zip his own pants. Yet he could play eight instruments and enjoyed a musical repertoire from country to classical of more than 7,000 pieces. Pieces that he played by ear with perfect pitch. What made the assignment a must-remember wasn't its strong narrative, but the three days I spent with photographer Henry Grossman.

Henry had photographed luminaries such as JFK, Robert Kennedy and opera singer Maria Callas for *Life* and other major magazines. Now he was turning his lens to Tony. Henry and I shared the same rental car and although we spent twelve-hour days with the subjects, we were totally caught up in the flow of our work and hardly spoke to one another. Occasionally Henry gave me a knowing look or a nod when Tony or Janice said or did something he thought notable.

But at the end of each long day, we stopped for coffee and compared our impressions. As a writer, I was telling the story of a mother and son through words. As a photographer, Henry was telling the story through images.

Henry described for me the vision he was seeing through his lens. "I'm seeing images of hands," he said. "Tony's hands reaching for the piano keys. But I'm also seeing Janice's hands. They're pressed against Tony's lips when he speaks too loudly. They're tapping him on the shoulder when he slips into an autistic rock. They're massaging his back as the doctor explains that no matter how hard Tony tries he will never read, he will never write."

These images, these compressed glimpses of the whole story as seen through his camera's lens, helped me do my job as a writer. They helped me answer what Hopkins professor Ted Gup calls the two eternal questions of all feature articles: What is the story about? And, what is the story about?

The answer to the first "What is the story about?" is simple. The story is about an autistic blind musical genius reared by a single mother. That's the question newspaper reporters answer.

The answer to the second "What is the story about?" distinguishes feature writers from reporters. This is what is really at the heart of the story, the human values behind the facts. The answer to this second question is more questions. How far will Janice's determination to help her son and Tony's talents take him? How complete can his metamorphosis be? Can Tony ever be free of autism's clutches?

Would I have conjured up these images if Henry had not alerted me to specific actions? Would the answer to the second question have been the same if Henry had not shared his thoughts with me? I'd like to think I would have returned to Maryland and figured it out, but it was pure joy to receive this manna from heaven.

Suppose Henry had spoken of images that I thought trivial. Or what if he came to conclusions from his side of the lens that I considered absurd. It wouldn't have mattered. The point is not to have a photographer, or anyone else, feed you the meaning of a story. This task is too critical to delegate. Getting the facts straight is essential, but putting them into the true context is divine.

The photographer's images as seen through the small frame of his camera's lens are intensified because the rest of the world is shut out. These images gain strength in number. One may be meaningless. But as you lovingly collect them, piece-by-piece, like your grandmother's Limoges, their sum becomes greater than their parts.

If you never meet up with a right-brained, articulate photographer you can still benefit from the creative edge of photography. You can create these images yourself. Simply shoot a few pictures. Quality is not important. The power of two-dimensional images differs from written or verbal images. Oskar Kokoschka, a pioneering modern painter of Viennese origin, explains visual orientation this way, "I have lived in space, not in time."

Snapshots help you to recreate the experience for yourself when you sit down to write. No matter how passionate you feel leaving an interview, life manages to fill in the valleys and level the peaks. To recapture the zest it helps to immerse yourself, using all your senses. Read your notes, listen to your tapes and look at the pictures. One Polaroid can evoke a rush of feeling. You can't produce the experience for the reader if you don't feel it yourself, viscerally. Recall Robert Frost's words, "No tears in the writer, no tears in the reader."

The second reason for you to snap a few shots is to use the images to detect relationships, patterns or contrasts in the piece. You may even spot new drama or tension you missed when reporting the story. The photos may lead you to insights you overlooked. They may even offer a whole new dimension on the story.

Andrew Ferguson, who was one of the producers of the "Children's Television Workshop," says for him a new work is never born with an idea. It's conceived from an image. On his way to work one day he spotted a group of black kids waiting on a corner for the bus to drive them to a white, suburban school. They were carrying their breakfast. He saw these kids in a tight little frame in his head and he began wondering about their lives and wondering about the issue of busing and a film was born. This can happen for you, too, when you open yourself to visual interpretation.

This reminds me of a conversation I had with our son Brad's, girlfriend Jenny. She mentioned how moved she was by her visit to the Holocaust museum in Washington, D.C. In the next breath we both zeroed in on the exhibit at the very end of the tour: a pile of leather shoes left behind by the victims before they were led into the incinerator. This image was not computer generated, nor did it have a single sound effect. It was poignant, it was simple, it was human. To us, it was the Holocaust.

No photo will automatically spell out the meaning of the story. That's up to you. The film, like the photographer, is one aid in pointing the way. The destination can be reached by many routes. This is just one.

If you forget your camera, you can still try visually exploring the story in your mind when you get back home. Roll up a piece of paper and look through it. What do you see? No, not the breakfast dishes. Look deeper to where you really live. What images form from your story? Where would you aim your camera? Would you use a wide-angle lens? What would it reveal? Now switch to a close-up lens, what would you hone in on? What drama, intimacy would these close-up shots show? Put these images together. Is a pattern emerging? What is it and what does it mean? What leaps can you make? Take a chance. Free associate.

Now call in the more critical left-side of your brain to pass judgement on the imaginative, intuitive judgments you just made. Do they hold up in light of the facts?

With this information as a guide, answer that second question. "What is the story about?"

I warned you, writing women's stories is never a straight shot. That's what makes it so compelling. But these strategies can help point you in the right direction. From there, what develops is all yours.

Picture This

A S READERS (AND WRITERS) of women's feature stories, we love images. It's the slow burn that stays with us long after a conversation ends, or the movie credits scroll down the screen or the book's cover closes. Just a mention of the image brings back the full power of the piece and we relive it again and again.

The Baltimore Sun published a six-part feature about a young woman who died of cancer, leaving behind a husband, a 7-year-old daughter and an unusual legacy. The series included myriad details of the woman's life and the spread of the disease itself. But one detail stood above all the others and made the story real for me.

While waiting for death, this mother wrote letters to her young daughter. She then asked a friend to give them to the child, one at a time, on those red-letter days in her life. To hand her a letter on those days when a daughter especially needs her mother: the day she goes on her first date, experiences her first love, her first heartbreak, her graduation, her wedding, her first career job, the birth of her children and the milestones in their lives.

I get chills every time I think of the friend doling out this mother's priceless words. I am certain no other gift this daughter will ever receive will be as treasured as these letters. I often wonder what influence these words will have on her as she grows into a woman. I wonder if she will live any differently because of them.

Reading a *Washington Post* review of the novel *Last Comes The Egg* my eyes stopped on a quote from the book. "A girl when she's born, well, in her belly, as a baby, she's got every egg she'll ever have! So, when you see a girl—any girl, even a bitsy baby—well, inside her she's got every egg that she'll ever make, every egg and all the life in her that she'll ever have. Which means…that even before you're born, you were always there with your mother. You were always there and you felt and knew everything."

Anyone who's taken eighth grade biology knows this. But did you ever stop to think about it, to consume the fact emotionally? I didn't until I came across that passage. Now when I glance at my sons—Scott, a computer consultant, Brad, a medical student and Ryan off to become a midshipman at the U.S. Naval Academy—I smile a secret smile. These now independent individuals were with me my first day of school. They couldn't have been closer as I dated my high school boyfriend, traipsed across Europe as a college student and married their father after graduation.

> ❧ *In every woman's story you write, strive to pinpoint an image or concept that will help the story live on in the reader's mind.*

Through the image of eggs, author Bruce Duffy touched me intimately. He made me think thoughts that have become part of my permanent inventory. Thoughts that may change, ever so slightly, how I think and act. Because of this I'm grateful to him and I'll remember his book.

In every woman's story you write, strive to pinpoint an image or concept that will help the story live on in the reader's mind.

When Kathy Scobee Fulgham, daughter of Dick Scobee, mission commander of the ill-fated Challenger space shuttle, told me she experiences recurring nightmares of her dad stranded on a cloud calling to her, "Kathy, Kathy, please help me," I knew I'd found an image that would help *Woman's Day* readers understand exactly what it was like for this young wife and mother to lose a dad she loved.

Some images can be humorous as well as poignant. When I spoke with Grace Corrigan, mother of Challenger's teacher-in-space Christa McAuliffe, she mentioned how she'd gotten a letter from a young boy from New Hampshire. He wrote that when he wanted to name his new baby goat Christa McAuliffe, his mother protested, "You can't name a goat Christa McAuliffe." But he held firm. "Christa was a winner and my goat's going to be a winner too," he pleaded.

Tucked inside the envelope sent to Grace was a photo of a now grown goat named Christa McAuliffe. The goat was resplendent in a wreath of blue ribbons.

These images are not restricted to feature stories. They're everywhere, in the books we read, the conversations we overhear, the movies we watch.

I dashed out in the middle of the movie *Mr. Holland's Opus* to write myself a note about the moment when Holland, a middle-aged music teacher played by Richard Dreyfus, tried to help his struggling music student find her stride.

"What do you like best about yourself?" he asked.

"My father says he likes my red hair," she replied.

"Why?"

"Because he says it reminds him of the sunset."

"Then play the sunset," Holland commanded.

Corny? No doubt. But I cried, not once, but both times I saw the movie. Memorable? I'll never forget its message, long after the detours of the plot haze over in my mind.

Once you become alert to images, they'll pounce on you as you interview, while you glance over your notes and as you reflect on your story and the people in it. Commit the image to your notebook, tack it above your computer, seal it in your soul.

I'm never sure what I'll do with these images as I rush to record them, to protect them from becoming a casualty of my imperfect memory. Yet, eventually something mysterious happens. After acknowledging how important they are to my writing, the precise opportunity appears for me to feed them to the reader. The moment seems so inspired that I can't imagine how the story could have been written without this phrase, this magical image.

But, while some of these images arrive ready to use, in the real world, others require assembly. Images may come disguised as lengthy quotes, a description of the story location, even a combination of objects for which you must supply the glue.

How these images arrive doesn't matter. All that's important is that you recognize them and include them so they can create for the reader vivid concepts and emotions that stay with her long after she's closed the magazine.

Gushing

ONE OF MY CLOSE FRIENDS, KATHY, has a 26-year-old daughter named Susan. Susan has breast cancer that has spread to her lungs. This young woman, newly married, is suffering one of life's grave injustices. And like all mothers, Kathy is suffering right along with her.

Being Kathy's friend, I listen as she tells me how her own priorities have changed. Months before, when the cancer was first diagnosed and optimistically thought to be contained in one breast, Kathy lamented that her daughter, anxious to have a honeymoon baby, would now have to wait until she was cancer free. "Five years," she said. "She might have to wait that long before they can begin trying." But when the whole sinister picture of the malignancy was fully exposed, Susan herself put the situation in focus, "Mom, now I'm not even thinking about having babies; I just want to live."

As Kathy tells me this, my heart breaks for Susan, Kathy, the whole family, even myself. I want to embrace Kathy. I want to shout out how rotten this world can be and, for a moment, casting aside my years of Catholicism, ask what *is* God thinking. But then I recall an aside Kathy made about a loving, well-intentioned relative who turned them off by gushing, yes, that's the word she used—gushing—and I hold my torrent of tears.

Kathy knew the woman meant well, but it wasn't what any of them needed. She didn't want this woman to expel her insides, evoking every adjective and adverb she'd ever heard. Superlatives are hard to swallow. Kathy longed for help in putting these emotional moments in context. Rather than exploring the drama through moans and groans, she wished her relative would examine its poignancy in relation to the rest the family. She wanted a third-person observer to breathe distance and perspective into their tragedy. Kathy yearned for the nouns and verbs, the pure hard-working parts of speech to help live life, not wallow in it.

So it is with readers.

Some assume, when they hear I write women's stories, that my copy is trimmed with lace and dotted with lipstick stains. In truth, it's coffee—decaf. They ask me how I can report on terminally ill children and not melt into maudlin prose. At first I wondered what they had been reading, but the comments persist—often from those who should know better. So the misconception that women's stories must drip with syrupy melodrama is out there. Maybe it's propagated by the tabloids. Surely not by the major women's magazines, the Seven Sisters, that are still rather restrained in how they portray raw emotion.

Please don't misconstrue. Editors today want the details, every last nuance that will make the event, no matter how tragic, come alive for the reader. It's been said that if you can make a New York editor cry, you've sold your story. I remember hearing Susan Ungaro, editor at *Family Circle*, speak about how the ante on this type of reporting has been raised. In the past, their magazine would not have placed the reader at the casket of a child, she said. But today, the reader must be there right beside the mother if the story is going to resonate for her.

Still, there's a way to position the reader without rubbing her face raw in the grief—without gushing. It seems to me that the more dramatic the story, the less fancy the writing has to be. You simply say what's happening in and out of your subject's mind without embellishing, without stretching, without searching for the soppy phrase or overly-emotional image. The key is restraint.

The saddest story I ever wrote, "The Greatest Gift of All," told the tragic tale of Sandy Barnes' 12-year-old son Richie who was killed by a bus as he rode his bike to school. It also told of a very special relationship that developed between Sandy and the young woman, Maria, whose life was saved by Sandy's decision to give her Richie's liver.

As a mother of three sons, one the age of Richie, the images, the language, the sentiment rushed out of my mind and on to the paper. But after the flood, I reined myself in. The reader wanted no part of my self-indulgence. She wanted the story to evoke her own emotions, not play hostess to mine. This is what I wrote.

> Sandy sat at her son's side throughout the night. Reaching for Richie's hand, she gently rubbed at the faded ink stains on his fingertips that remained from a school project. Occasionally she'd feel him twitch and wonder, "Did he squeeze my hand?" But as the hours passed, she began to recognize these movements as im-

plicit muscle spasms. With dawn approaching, Sandy's mind was beginning to accept what her heart still refused to acknowledge. Her thoughts drifted back to one afternoon a year earlier, as she was signing the donor release statement on her new driver's license. When she told Richie what she was doing, he mumbled, "How gross."

But she explained that if she weren't alive anymore and someone needed her organs to live, it would be a waste for *both* people to die. He agreed. Then he asked, "When I get my license, will you witness it so I can be an organ donor?"

Writing about emotional moments is like sharing an experience with a friend. As you write, hold her image tightly in front of your mind. Imagine how your friend's reacting. Is she grimacing? Did she cringe? It's okay, as long as she's still with you. But if you glimpse her looking away, then tone it down. Understate.

Consider these parts of the piece that I'd write differently today. Here's a passage explaining how Maria learned of Richie's death.

The transplant coordinator wrote to Maria Lara about Sandy and Richie and included Sandy's address and phone number. Every day since her transplant, Maria had reflected on the nameless child whose liver was keeping her alive. Now with the details of Richie's tragic tale before her, Maria was moved to tears.

I'd rewrite the last sentence this way:

Now with the details of Richie's death before her, Maria wept.

Later:

Finally, nearly a year after her transplant, she faced her fears head-on. She chose a simple card and, agonizing over every word, wrote...

Now try this. Rewrite the two sentences above, letting the facts speak for themselves. Then compare them with what I've done below. You may prefer yours, that's fine.

Ready? Here's my take.

> Nearly a year after her transplant, she chose a simple card and wrote...

Try another:

> A month later, Maria called Sandy and assured her that she was doing well. She asked all about Richie. While Maria felt uneasy speaking to this woman from whose loss she had gained so much, Sandy was thrilled. To her, this was living proof that the transplant had been a success.

Ready?

Here's mine. I cut, *from whose loss she had gained so much.* Yuck. Melodramatic.

And finally, the ending read:

> Running to greet "Grandma Sandy" on a recent visit, Richie, now 2, gives her a big hug. Seeing the love between them, Maria says something she never forgets, "If it weren't for Richie and you, I wouldn't be here and neither would my boys. I can never thank you enough."

Finished?

OK, here's mine. I cut, *Seeing the love between them, Maria says something she never forgets.* This is implicit in the story itself. Saying it borders on sap.

Every time you write about moments of human experience filled with pathos, cut the sentiments. Real emotions need no amplification. Get out of the way and let the power of the details carry the message. Give this to the reader and she'll shed tears of her own—and be happy about them.

Quick Switch

WHEN THE STORY OF GARY CHENOWETH, the single father of two young sons—one with a dozen brain tumors and the other with a hole in his heart—appeared in *Family Circle*, reader response was overwhelming.

Seems like readers love to cry, you say. But there was more to writing "Father Love" than stringing pearls of pity. Unfortunately, I didn't learn that until after a second rewrite. The lesson the editor taught me has salvaged many of my sagas since, so it might just help you too.

"I can't take it anymore," my editor whined into the phone. (Yes, she's the same woman who took the scalpel to that first *Family Circle* drama, an editor who can be as tactless as she is creative, intuitive and talented.) "It's a great story, but something's wrong; I don't know, it's just so sad. Readers will never stand for it."

"This man must do *something* besides work and care for these kids," she said, her voice rising and falling with the inflection on *something*. Truth is, he didn't. All his waking hours involved doctors' appointments, medications and therapists. A hot time for him was taking the boys to a Make-A-Wish Foundation holiday party. No wonder his Harley Davidson rusted.

Silently I pouted. Writers work hard to get their subjects to slobber and then when they do, we're told to mind our manners and tone it down.

On a deeper level I knew the editor was on to something. I remembered reading about a very successful diet that required you on day one to stock your refrigerator with gallons of ice cream, the rich fatty kind, and pizza topped with extra cheese and sausage. Then fill your cupboard with super-sized bags of greasy potato chips and anything else you craved. Day two you started eating all you wanted. When you felt full, you were encouraged to eat more. Day three, ditto. Day four, the same. By day five you notice your stomach's protruding and you pray it's not permanent. The lure of the hot fudge sundae begins to wane, but the fries still appeal. By day six, you're sure your stomach will turn inside out if you swallow one more ounce of fat. And by day seven, well, you get the point. I've always been too timorous to give it a try, afraid that I might be the only woman who, after a week of gorging, still can't eat just one chip. But I understood the principle, too much of a good thing. Same with emotion.

All the editor longed for was a slice of comic relief. The story was too heartbreaking. It read like a purge. Like a Lenten season when you gave up candy, movies and talking about sex. The reader wants to cheat just a bit, like sneaking a bite of a Milky Way on Good Friday. And unless we allow her some slack, she just might put the magazine down.

There had to be an answer but, like Gary's life, it wasn't simple. In the end, the answer was found within the story itself. One night I asked Gary if he ever had a moment of sheer craziness. "Was there ever a time you said to yourself, What the heck, let's live?"

Gary thought and thought. When his answer came, of course, his sons were in every word. Looking back, it seems quite mild. But it was all we had and it worked.

> With all the daily pressures, the Chenoweths still had their moments of joy—even abandon. One Sunday night Gary and the boys were driving to a restaurant for dinner when Lacy spotted a sign for an ocean resort 147 miles away. "Let's go," he begged.
>
> "Come on, Dad," Gary Jr. pleaded.
>
> The sun was already setting, the air was getting chilly and there was school the next day. "No way, not now," Gary said, then reconsidered, "OK. What the heck."
>
> There was a full moon that night as Gary carried his 100-pound older son across the beach and down to the Atlantic Ocean. Gary Jr. laughed in delight as the water lapped over his toes.
>
> "Sure it was crazy," Gary admits, "but worth it. I have to show them the world out there can be a happy place."

This was all we needed. A respite between a succession of problems. A time for the reader to catch her breath, to smile. A tone break tends to be tricky and beginning writers are told not to do it. "Keep a consistent tone," is an axiom chiseled into our minds along with "brush your teeth, say your prayers and change your underwear everyday just in case...." To become a better writer you must risk, because if your story is emotion-packed you have no choice.

The key to varying the tone is to make the quick switch believable. You do this by staying true to the subject's character. Gary didn't take up with a prostitute, for instance, nor did he trek to Atlantic City to gamble. But he did, on a whim, turn his car around and drive his sons nearly three hours to the ocean, when it was cold and getting dark, and they had school the next morning. All for a moment's glee.

This is as crazy as Gary gets. But he needed it, the boys needed it and most important, the reader needed it. What a clever editor.

The Main Event

Spilling Words onto Paper

WRITING AN ARTICLE OR FEATURE STORY is like making a souffle. You can mix all the ingredients, but unless you whip it with air it'll never rise.

One of our feminine wiles—men, you're invited to borrow it, interest free—is viewing ideas holistically. We envision an embryonic thought as a magazine coverline. We "see" the published article, our words framing photos, our sidebars buttressing the page and our byline in big letters—all before we begin organizing and categorizing what we will need to write the piece.

On the other hand, men typically build an idea in their mind: lead, quote, germ of the story, points to prove, closing. Logical. Linear. And occasionally lackluster. No wonder they can't follow our thoughts when we make those giant but outrageously creative leaps in conversation.

Holistic thinking encourages us to explore all the possibilities of an idea. It lays a smorgasbord of facts at our feet, allowing us to nibble and choose. Men might benefit from trying this sweeping, feminine approach when casting for article ideas. In return, we women can measure our often grandiose, and sometimes unrealistic, concepts against their more masculine literal yardstick.

A second feminine wile that helps us write is our love of daydreams. You may have considered daydreaming naughty, but no more. Imagine yourself coming up with a great idea, pitching it to an editor, getting an assignment, writing the story, seeing it published. Visualizing puts the subconscious on notice to work overtime to make this notion real.

Women writers have a third wile at work, emotion. For years we've been encouraged to downplay this aspect of our nature. What matters is our intellect, we've been told. If it can't be found in a book or doesn't come from an expert, what good is it? This is even more so for men. Have you ever heard of a man who measured his masculinity by the size of his emotional quotient?

The time's come for both sexes to acknowledge emotion as a potent force for all types of articles we write—whether life and death dramas, deep first person essays or information-driven pieces like how to beat stress. And once we unleash this emotional nature into our writing, probing the feelings of the people whose stories we tell and our own reaction to their trials, our articles will gain new depth.

How do you explore all possible angles of an idea and massage it until it's emotion packed? How can you instill the deeper meaning to the notion?

First, you must calm yourself. Try breathing deeply and allowing yourself the time to think, to create. This is hard work. You'll want to jump up and pour a third cup of coffee. You'll insist on checking for the mail again. You may even succumb to putting in a load of wash. Resist. Belt yourself to your chair.

Now that you've settled down, the chorus of naysayers in your head start up. They tell you you have nothing worthwhile to say and if you let them carry on you'll believe them.

Replace them with what I call your Second Self. This is the persona you assume, the character you become, when you sit down to write. When an article really reaches a reader, it's usually because the writer herself has come through in the words on the page—even if she never once referred to herself. Her personality as a narrator is so strong that she, herself, becomes a character in the article, no matter what it's about.

When the reader puts down such an article, she knows more than facts, she knows the writer too. She hears the frog in the writer's voice as she *speaks* the words, sees the freckle on her pug nose and even smells the lingering scent of vanilla cologne. If you finish reading an article and the image of its writer is pale, chances are the article itself made an equally flimsy impression.

How can you puff yourself up to assume the tall, erect, authoritative posture of a writer with something to say? For some it helps to read a few passages that *shout* from the page, or listen to classical music or an inspiring self-help tape. For others, props work. One writer finds Banana Republic khakis and a white shirt kick in her "I've got something to say" mood—ever since she saw a photo of Hemingway dressed similarly. For another the transformation is sensual, occurring when she removes her notes from her soft, tan leather journal. A third writer visualizes herself strong-voiced, confident and opinionated, tapping out incredibly insightful concepts. Other writers report they imagine themselves to be a writer they admire. Assuming the mind of that person frees them from responsibility for what appears on the page, and the results can be astonishing.

Once you're firmly fixed in your writing persona, take your story idea and go deep within yourself. It might help to picture this idea written on a tiny piece of paper, the kind you get in a fortune cookie. Now turn the paper, twist it, examine it from all angles. What can you add to the idea? What ways can it be handled? How about your feelings? What gut response do you have to the idea? Now hold it up to the light. What does it mean to your readers? How do you suppose they'll react?

It's natural for you to probe your thoughts and to roll things over in your mind. But if your viewpoint's been undervalued in the past, you'll have to work doubly hard to hear what you're thinking.

This is what will happen. Upstairs, the cameras will roll. Be alert, because there may not be a drum roll. And there won't be a super-sized box of buttered popcorn waiting. For me, the preview comes with some frames undeveloped while others lie cut on the production floor. There may be a beginning, a middle and an end, but this is rare. Usually at least one part's missing. For you it may be different. I glimpse moments, incidents or events. Sometimes I have no notion where they'll fit, if anywhere. But because they rise out of the mountains of notes I've amassed, I suspect they've got heart and I try to pay attention. I play with these images like a kitten with string, twirling them, following them to see where they lead. I look for relationships, patterns, contrasts, and I ask myself what metaphors they bring to mind. At this point I tell my logical, literal nature to back off, allowing the freewheeling, right-side of my brain to party.

You and I could be given the same information and, after we probe it and piece it, what you make of it might be totally different from what I come up with—and that's the way it should be.

At this point you should have a general picture in your mind of where you're going with this story. Got it? Good. Now rein in your wild and woolly digressions. Check your incredibly creative storyline to see if it meets every reader's question, "What's in it for me?"

If your idea meets this criteria, assign the story a deadline. Call in your linear thinking troops, those guys you shooed from your mind when you were coming up with this great take. With their help, determine the points that will develop the story so it gives the reader the payoff she's looking for.

🐞 🐞 🐞

"But *how* do you write?" my students plead. "It's easy to talk *about* writing, but what do we do when we sit down face-to-face with a blank page, an empty screen or worse, an empty mind?"

Believe me, this is a question I understand. I've experienced many false starts...and no-starts. The following is what works for me. Try it when your writing is stalled and needs a jump.

You know why I like this system so much? You never have to write those anal outlines that your fifth grade teacher demanded. In fact, you don't waste a minute copying anything. Then when you do write the story itself you feel as if the muse is directing your hand. And no matter what type of feature article you're writing—whether it's a true life drama, an informative piece, a how-to or a relationship piece— it comes out full-bodied, with rounded edges and no jagged parts. It's hard to make writing more pain-free.

Step one

Let's say you've used your feminine wiles to come up with a super idea and you've pitched an editor and gotten the assignment, or maybe you've decided to write the piece on spec. Either way, you've taken step one. Now place the cloak of your Second Self over your shoulders and take step two.

Step two

Take notes as you research and interview, leaving a wide margin on the right hand side of the pad. When you're finished, get in a totally relaxed mood and reread all your notes, every last one.

If you gathered newspaper clippings or other material read that again too. Look at the pictures. Listen to the taped interviews. Do whatever you can to recreate the experience. Don't force a thing. Let feelings, impressions and first thoughts come naturally.

Then do it all over again. This time be alert to an anecdote that might make a lead, a quote that shows insight or an image that brings it home for the reader. When you see something you want to use in your story, mark a word or two in the margin to remind you. For instance, the words "Roper/health" will bring back to me the gist of an interview with a doctor who says women should schedule playtime to stay healthy. Or you might just write "Sue/lead" meaning this anecdote about Sue might work for the lead.

After you've gone all through your notes, copy (I *know* I told you no copying, but this is short, you'll see.) the slugs that are in the margin of your pads on a large sheet of paper. Study them. What relationships do you see? Any patterns? Any contradictions? What do the words suggest? What you're looking for here is the big picture. Since you're a good writer, and thought about your story before this, you probably know what your take, or point of view, will be. But now that you have a smorgasbord of information before you, you might find some surprises.

Now number the slugs in the order that you're going to write them. How do you know? Always look to your reader for answers. Ask yourself, What does my reader want to know, and when does she want to know it? This is your *outline*. Now put your notes away—and don't peek.

Step three

Before you put your fingers to the keys do one more thing. Read. Read something for 10 or 15 minutes that's written in the tone and voice in which you want to write. The article or book you choose may be something you or someone else has written. The point is, it should be writing you want to emulate, writing that fits the publication you're targeting. (You might want to read an article similar to yours in *that* publication.)

OK, you're ready. This is the fun part. You've done all the thinking. Now freewrite. Put your mind on auto pilot and hold on for the ride. With only the outline in front of you, begin to write and don't stop until you've finished. Later you can go back and edit or correct the spelling or whatever.

If you have a hard time starting, imagine a friend asking, "Sally, what story are you working on?" You wouldn't run to check your notes before you answered, you'd just tell her. And that's exactly what you should do.

Yankee Moxie

AFTER WE MOVED FROM NEW HAMPSHIRE to Maryland I was out walking one afternoon with our youngest son Ryan when a neighbor joined us. She spoke excitedly about finding a watercolor painting, beautifully framed, in an old trunk in her mother's house. As she described the East Hampton shore line in muted shades, I couldn't wait to see the painting.

"Where did you hang it?" I asked.

"Oh, it's not up yet," she snapped. "My decorator hasn't OK'd the spot."

Was I hearing right? She really wouldn't hang a painting without permission? From that moment, I knew I'd entered a different world, one with an odd fit—at least for me.

New England Yankees are seemingly intimidated by nothing. If there's a job to be done they'll pick the brain of someone who has done it, borrow a how-to book or just hack away, trial and error, until they get it right—or nearly so. They're not paralyzed by perfection. They aim high, fall a little short and celebrate very good.

I know I am stereotyping people, pigeonholing according to geography, and I apologize. But it seems to me that residents a few states apart share time zones but not attitude. Saturday nights in New Hampshire found friends gathered around a woodstove speaking of mammoth home restorations. Sometimes you wondered why they didn't raze the place and start anew.

The point is, Yankees, by chance or by choice, weren't left worshipful of experts bearing letters after their names. They were inspired by those with single-minded vision to decide what had to be done, scoop out a plan and do it—whether the plan was to remove a load-bearing wall, deliver a baby or scale Mount Washington.

So it is with writing.

The best writing is done with a can-do attitude. It's that hint of moxie, a dose of self-importance and a belief that your point of view matters. These healthy self-assertions don't always come easily. Still if you repeat them often enough you start to believe them.

In writing feature stories, a cocktail of knowledge and moxie comes in handy from the get-go. To write a great story, you must believe you're up to it.

When students ask me what's the most important thing I can tell them about writing for women, I turn to Jane Harrigan of *The Editorial Eye*: "The story is not in my notes. The story is in my head." The students sit there, collectively holding their breath, pens poised, waiting for something more.

"That's it?" their eyes ask. "Nothing more?"

"Write it down," I tell them. Then read it every Monday morning for a year so you can't forget it.

When I first wrote for newspapers, I raced out to cover a story, filling my notebook with facts and quotes. Then back at the paper, I'd punch out a creative lead, fill in the middle with information and close with a flourish.

If you write like this your stories will be published, you will be paid and life won't be bad. But you'll also never wake early raring to get your thoughts down on paper. Instead you'll wait passively to be spoon-fed the story, taking down what everyone else tells you, instead of digging deep within yourself to figure out where all the pieces fit and what they mean to you and the reader.

I once wrote what was supposed to be a news story about an embattled school superintendent in our small New England town who doled out teaching assignments in exchange for feminine favors. The town tolerated his antics until he went so far as to replace a much-loved kindergarten teacher with his favored fling. I was enraged. My piece tore him to shreds. It ran on the front page and was slugged "analysis."

Every feature story should be a gift to the reader of the writer's passionate point of view. Never write without it.

The Little Black Dress

WHEN YOU WANT TO WRITE A FEATURE STORY that isn't a true life drama, or a service piece, or even an article on relationships, you might want to consider what I call the Little Black Dress of article formulas. This formula, also known as the *Wall Street Journal* formula (although the *Journal* insists there's no such thing), is as versatile as the little black dress. It's always appropriate, always classy. You can embellish it with your personal touches or wear it plain. Either way, tuck it in your bag and take it out anytime.

This formula has seven parts: the lead, the high quote, the nut graph, the buttress point, the developmental points, the background and the closing. (Don't worry if you don't recognize the jargon, I'll explain it as we go along.)

The lead

The lead is the first few sentences or paragraphs. What type of lead do you think readers like best? If you guessed the anecdote, you're right. Readers say they like the little story that casts a light on the bigger story. Using an anecdote always draws a reader in, but be sure the reader can relate. If your anecdote involves a woman, can your reader imagine herself being that woman? Can she identify with what's happening to her? And, of course, no matter how cunning the anecdote, it won't work unless it's true to the rest of the article in content and tone.

Like anything else, anecdotes can be overdone. You may not want to start *every* article with an anecdote. Maybe you'd like to begin with a scene or an intriguing statement. Asking a question used to be high on the list of writers' favorite leads. But it suffered from over popularity. So judge for yourself.

Many writers favor quotes as an entrée to their pieces. Yet an editor once asked how a reader could be expected to care what someone's saying if she doesn't know who was saying it and doesn't know what the story is about. He's right. Unless a quote is so evocative it will overcome these obstacles, save it for later.

Points to ponder about leads: First, a lead should show reader identification, mirroring the reader so she sees herself or something that interests or affects her in the first few sentences. Second, the lead should promise the reader information, entertainment or inspiration—ideally two or three of the three. And you win another bonus point if the lead introduces some intrigue to get the reader wondering.

The high quote

Soon after the lead, but not necessarily the next sentence, comes a quotation. Placing a quote high up in the article helps to pull the reader into the story by letting her hear your subject's voice early on. After all, who can resist eavesdropping?

Some quotes offer figures or facts, but the best ones, those that linger with the reader, go beyond the basics deep into the speaker's psyche. They offer insight into her. Generally, quotes should be short and pithy.

Remember to set up your quotes by preceding them with a line or two of background that will help the reader appreciate the speaker's words.

The nut graph

This is old journalism shorthand for "in a nut shell" meaning what the article is all about. Here, in a few sentences, you tell the reader why she's reading the article. You put your arms around the piece, giving her the big picture. For instance, if you're writing about baby boomer mothers going to college with their kids and your lead profiles a mother and daughter who are roommates at a large state university, your nut graph might give the big picture of how many colleges across the country have parents studying alongside their children and what effect experts say this has—if it's important—on the student's college experience. The nut graph might also mention any news peg or connection your story has with something that's happening now and is in the public's consciousness. For instance, the news peg for the story about boomers returning to school with their kids could be recently enacted enticements of reduced tuition for parent/child study partners.

The buttress point

Then we move along to the points that prove the promise made in the lead and explained in the nut graph. The first point, known as the buttress point, comes right below the nut graph. It is the engine that will drive the story in a specific direction.

This is a critical junction in the article. It is here the reader decides to continue reading or decides to watch daytime television. Give some thought to the point you choose to make here. Experiment with moving the various points in your article up to the position of the buttress point. Notice how the emphasis of the story changes.

If I think my reader may be skeptical of what I'm saying, I'll make the buttress point my strongest argument. But, if I sense the reader is with me from the lead, I'll save the most convincing fact for the end.

The developmental points

Next come the developmental points. A developmental point is additional information that broadens the article and supports the theme outlined in the nut graph. You can write a feature article with a dozen points—and *The Wall Street Journal* often does—but you probably need a minimum of three to tell the story or convince the reader.

Perhaps you'll use a quote from an expert as a developmental point. Readers like experts with letters after their names if you're writing about a medical issue or other highly specialized material. But they also like to hear from their sisters (and brothers) in the trenches, those with life experiences. If you're writing about rearing drug free kids and a mother brought up four in the most crime-infested part of the city, her credibility's on a par with any Ph.D. holder.

Occasionally throw in a new study or a statistic, but always pad it with people. Never let the information become a data dump that squeezes the air out of the feature, turning it into a term paper.

Let me add a few words about transitions. Anytime you present a new block of information, you must build a tram for the reader to deliver her to the next informational gate. Nonfiction guru John McPhee says that well written articles don't need transitions, their structures are organic. Well, that's fine for John McPhee, but for you and me, we may need a little help moving our readers along. If you need help crafting a smooth transition, try "talking" the piece. Read it out loud, pretending you are speaking to a friend. How would you say it to be sure she understood?

The joy of transitions is the chance they give the writer to express her opinion and shore up her point of view. When students ask how they can get their voice into a story, I point to transitions.

When I wrote about Ringo, a cat with a nose for danger, I began by describing his owners, Carol and Ray Steiner, and the mysterious illness they had suffered. I mentioned that they were so weak and fatigued they could barely care for their 26-pound red tabby, Manx. Then I spoke of the culprit: a deadly methane gas leak below the foundation of the Steiner's home that was poisoning the couple. Transitioning to the next block of information—Ringo's discovery of the deadly fumes—I wrote:

> Then something incredible happened—and the Steiners believe it saved their lives.
> Ringo, who'd just come in from the yard, began flinging himself against the front door.

The story could have been told without that first sentence of transition. The facts would have stayed the same and the reader would have learned what happened. But the reader wouldn't have *experienced* the story without those few judgmental words.

The background

Let's get back to the formula. We've talked about the lead, the pithy quote high in the story, the nut graph, the buttress point and the developmental points that follow. Now with most feature articles you'll come across background or history that should be included.

In the story about parents and children going to college together, you might explain that this trend began with the wife of a college admissions officer who was suffering from the empty-nest syndrome.

If the background material is important, consider moving it up as your lead or just below it.

The closing

The closing, or ending, is your chance to nail your message in the reader's mind. Some of the best endings catch the reader by surprise. What you don't want to do with an ending is to summarize everything that's been said. You also don't want to drag it out like the last guests at your party who say they're leaving then stand in the doorway for another half-hour.

Wrap it all up by circling back to the lead and finishing an anecdote that you began there or by referring to something mentioned high up. Or glance into the crystal ball and suggest where the story could go from here. Or, my favorite, end with a poignant quote that says exactly the thought you want to leave with the reader.

Never Listen to an Editor

A WHILE BACK, A WRITER FRIEND PHONED sounding dejected.

"Just listen to this," she said reading a rejection letter she'd received from a *Woman's Day* editor relating to a piece on cleaning everything better and quicker. The story was submitted on speculation. It was based on a class taught at a local community college by an instructor named The Queen of Clean. The article offered a fresh solution to a stale problem: housework. While this topic may not grab you, it did the editor—at least at first.

Buoyed by the editor's initial interest, my friend worked hard on the piece, interviewing, writing, rewriting.

When the rejection arrived, saying only that the article wasn't what they hoped for, my friend was near tears. But she composed herself long enough to retrieve the original query. She read to me what she had promised in the proposal, then she read me the finished piece.

"What's different?" she asked. "Tell me, what did I do wrong?"

I knew she wanted honesty, no matter how hard it was to swallow. But the truth was, she did nothing wrong.

Let me explain. When she wrote the article, she followed her query to the letter. She promised to show readers how to clean a kitchen in 20 minutes flat, and she did. She promised to tell how one household cleanser can work for bed, bath and beyond, and she did that too. So what went so awry that the editor didn't even ask for a rewrite? Read on.

Later it happened again to this same writer. This time the rejection came from the new editor of a regional magazine that had published my friend's stories several times. And this time it was an assignment that went bad, not just an article on speculation. In fact, the editor had sent my friend a detailed assignment letter outlining, point-by-point, what she wanted covered in the feature article. Again, my friend did exactly as she was told. So when the article was rejected, she lost it. She picked up the phone and, in an exasperated tone, read to the editor her own assignment letter. She stopped at every point the editor requested and plugged in the part of the article that answered it.

"So why don't you like it? she asked. "I did everything you said."

What the editor said next should be tattooed to the back of every freelance writer's hand: "Never listen to an editor." Then she explained, "you're the one experiencing the story. We're not with you when you go into the trenches to research a story so we can't tell you what to write. We can only tell you to bring us back something more."

Now therein lies the key: something more.

My friend was doing nothing wrong, but she wasn't doing enough right. Editors will say they don't want surprises. They want to know what to expect from a piece. True. They don't want less than you promised, but they don't want precisely what you promised either. They want more than you promised. Make the article better than the query. Make it passionate. Make it evocative. Make it dazzling. Write with panache.

An editor, like any reader, reads to discover something. If there's nothing new in the article than what was promised in the query, she's disappointed. (And it won't be long before you will be too.) It's like a Christmas with no surprises. So uncover the gems that you couldn't possibly have known when you proposed the story, then wrap them up in beautiful prose. Give 'em what you promised, then give 'em more. Lots more.

Reader's Digest's Secret Formula

THE STRUCTURE FOR WRITING A TRUE LIFE DRAMA is as individual as the subject herself. Each woman, each dilemma, each take-home message for the reader is unique. So putting a formula to such a life experience is a little like convincing a new mother that her baby is like every other baby because each has two arms and two legs and cries a lot. It can't be done.

But you know what can be done—especially if you've sat for a half hour, chewed your pen and bit your acrylic nail and still haven't come up with a workable formula? You can start with this one. It comes from a giant, *Reader's Digest,* so you can trust that it's been proven— every month in their "Drama in Real Life."

Use this only as a springboard to your own structures for telling women's true stories, don't get addicted to it. And let me warn you, once you learn this formula you'll never—and I mean never—read one of these stories the same way.

Here are the five easy pieces of a *Reader's Digest* drama. The letters spell out SCAMP, each one a section of the story. Let's make up a story and see how it comes together.

"S" stands for setting

Our drama is about three women who decide to spend a Saturday afternoon sailing an O'Day off the shores of East Hampton, Long Island. We open the story by putting our reader on a smooth sandy bank at the water's edge near a picturesque town of gray shingled houses with window boxes sprouting red geraniums. We introduce the three women to our reader by having them interact with the environment in a meaningful way. For instance, the reader sees Shirley, a sailing instructor, hoisting the mast as the wind gently grazes her cheek. Her friend, Beverly, an animal rights activist, stores a few extra sodas in the cooler before handing it to Martha, a single mom.

Next comes "C" for character

Although the reader knows from the lead who the women are, she must identify with them and care desperately what happens to them or she'll never feel compelled to read to the end. To do this, you develop these women by fleshing out a few well-chosen details. For instance, we learn that this is instructor Shirley's first sail since she learned her breast cancer was in remission. In fact, we hear her say that this is a "celebratory voyage." Next, we eavesdrop as Beverly speaks of the elaborate arrangements she made with friends to care for her brood of pets to get the afternoon free. And when single-mom Martha is asked why her young son didn't join them, she tells us that when she went to wake him he was sleeping so soundly that "something seemed to stop my hand midair. He'll join us next time," she says. By now the reader's involved in these women's lives. She identifies with at least one of them.

"A" for action

The secret here is what is at stake. The more the better. Let me explain. Suppose you're writing about a middle-aged woman who has a great family, a great job, even a great bonsai—yet she's not happy: Her breasts sag. So one night in the wee hours as she sits in front of the television exercising her breasts and massaging them with $50 an ounce cream, an infomercial comes on showing women who swear to have sung Happy 40th Birthday years ago strut across the screen with breasts as taunt as steel cylinders—thanks to the miracle hands (and knife) of plastic surgeon Dr. Delight. Before sunrise our subject has signed up for plastic surgery. Up to now our reader might sympathize with her. But unless she herself has breasts en route to Key West, she's not going to feel compelled to find out what happens next. Who cares?

Now imagine the difference in the *Digest* drama in which I wrote about the toddler lost in the desert for four days. Here was a baby in danger of dying alone. See what I mean?

Of course you can't always find these baby-in-jeopardy stories so you have to work with what you've got. Just be sure you have a sympathetic subject in an awful predicament—through no fault of her own.

OK. Back to our three women sailors. In the action part of the formula, they go out into the sound and a wind out of nowhere (rough weather was not forecast) kicks up. They try to tack, but suddenly a giant wave capsizes their boat and they find themselves catapulted into the still icy spring waters.

In this midsection you need to develop the peaks and valleys of the story. The higher the peaks and the lower the valleys the better. At first one woman is trapped under the boat and for a few moments becomes disoriented. The reader realizes she's in danger of drowning (valley). But the woman's smart, she composes herself, she watches the bubbles rising to learn which direction is up. Reunited on the surface, the three women become chilled and begin to worry, but then they spy a trawler a few hundred feet away and wave to alert the captain (peak). Unfortunately the boat turns, oblivious to the women's dilemma (valley). The women create life preservers out of their clothing. They tell stories to keep their minds occupied (peak). But when the sun sets and temperatures plummet, each silently wonders how long she can hang on (valley). Suddenly they hear the sputter of a motor boat and they rejoice and so does the reader (peak). But then the sound becomes dimmer and dimmer until they're left with only the sound of lapping waves against their sinking boat (valley). Understand? Ups and downs. Two caveats: The women can't be stupid and they must use their brains or their brawn to get themselves out of their mess.

"M," the metanoia

This fourth part is the moment when the women realize their problem will be solved They will be rescued, they won't die eight miles from shore. In this case, I'm going to cop out and allow a Coast Guard helicopter to pluck them from the sea. So the metanoia, or the moment of insight, is when they see the helicopter descending towards them.

This moment should not happen until the trio has proven to our reader that they're smart, feisty and spiritual women. This last point, spirituality, used to be reserved for religious publications and *Reader's Digest.* No longer. Angels are appearing everywhere. It's a miracle when we read a story that doesn't embrace an other-world dimension. And it's a trend that watchers say will be with us well into the next century. In our story, the women prayed for God's help. We even overhear Martha thanking God for sparing her young son from joining them on the sail.

And, at the end, the "P" for postlude

The postlude is the doggie bag, the take home message for the reader. In our story the postlude implies that God is watching. Remember Martha's comment that "something seemed to stop my hand midair," and that if you persevere and have faith you can overcome anything, even giant waves that appear out of nowhere. In the best stories, the message is a whisper between writer and reader. In the worst stories, it's a pedantic school teacher making you repeat after her. Follow the first four steps, the fifth is a gift to both you and the reader.

❦ ❦ ❦

OK, now that you know *Reader's Digest's* secret formula, take a copy of a *Digest* "Drama In Real Life" and highlight each of its five parts. Do this with feature stories in other magazines and newspapers, especially those that you find particularly riveting. Even do it with a story or two you've written. Mark them up, still better, cut up the sections then put them back together like a puzzle. Do this often enough and you'll start to recognize structure in every story you read. No matter how seamlessly the author constructed the plot, it will become a blueprint to you. And this is good. There's no better way to learn how to construct a story.

Relationships

NOT LONG AGO RELATIONSHIP ARTICLES fell into disfavor with some magazine editors. Although they suspected many women thrived on these pieces, they still believed if they included these stories in their lineup their magazine wouldn't be taken seriously. And they probably had a point.

Then another problem developed. Relationship articles became preachy, moralistic, written in the voice of God. The articles all seemed the same—no matter when or where they were published. They appeared formulaic and seemed to rehash the same he-did, she-did anecdotes. The quotes all seemed to come from the same tired authorities. Even worse, the articles treated the reader as brainless, taking 10 pages to spell out what a reader could conclude in one.

Readers revolted. They wanted relationship articles that were thoughtful, sensitive and compelling. They wanted to be spoken to in an intelligent voice, and they wanted the words supported by a workable structure.

While every article is unique, there are specifics you can use to strengthen your relationship pieces. Here are a few.

Tell a bona fide story—not a veiled lecture—of a couple experiencing a challenge to their relationship. Create a sense of mystery by getting the reader to ask herself, "Will they stay together or will they break up?" Ask a qualified counselor to assess their situation, making implicit comments about the stress to their relationship, their communication styles and other pertinent factors.

Although relationship topics are perennials—jealousy, anger, competition and heartbreak—give them a new spin by finding a current hook or angle. For instance, current surveys about women marrying later might be a starting point. Even academic studies can produce an updated twist, such as up-to-date research that shows monogamy is good for your immune system. Popular entertainment often reintroduces classic subjects. Consider all that was written about female bonding after the movie *Thelma and Louise* or the exploration of obsessive love following *Fatal Attraction*. The popular sitcom "Seinfeld" was an oft-used point of departure for a look at friendships between men and women.

Including a quiz at the end of the story that engages the reader by asking her vital, psychological questions will add substance to your piece. For instance, when I wrote "Marriage Prep 101" for *For The Bride,* I ended with a half-dozen questions that the reader and her fiance could answer together to gauge how prepared they are for marriage's big issues.

Questions included: How often did each partner expect to have sex? Would they have joint or separate bank accounts? How about children? How many? When? And with whose parents would they spend the holidays? Scoring was easy and readers were told what their answers meant.

"The Serious Art of Playing" for *Bride's Magazine* told how a sense of fun is vital to a happy marriage. Instead of a quiz per se, I ended the article with seven suggestions for playful activities. My suggestions ranged from keeping a journal chronicling your life together, to buying a few favorite toys such as kites to fly together or squirt guns for water fights.

Another way to strengthen your article is to end with a list that makes advice more definitive and accessible to readers. Best yet, number the list: "10 Ways To Pillow Talk With Your Husband." The numbers make great coverlines for the magazines too.

How Not to Fix a Broken Toaster

WRITING AN ARTICLE ABOUT HOW TO FIX A RUSTY, two-slice toaster with a crumb door that sticks won't endear you to editors—nor will it get you published. If a reader doesn't care to learn what you want to teach her—she'd rather just pitch that toaster and buy a new one—you can cartwheel brilliant phrases within golden prose and you still won't pry a yes from the editor's lips.

But don't shy away from service (how-to) pieces. This hard-working article type, which teaches readers everything from how to forge better relationships, to how to create a stock portfolio, is a favorite with readers. What's wonderful about service articles, for the reader, is they come guilt-free. She doesn't suffer pangs of conscience for not making dinner or returning friends' calls because she's learning something.

Editors love them too. How-to pieces, along with true life dramas, are the easiest types of articles to sell. Ever notice how editors devote the drawingest part of their magazine cover, the upper left hand corner, to these how-to titles?

Here are a few things to keep in mind when you write them.

Find the right topic

Be sure the topic's enticing. No rusty toasters.

The topic needs to be relevant to the publication's reader. You wouldn't expect *Modern Bride* to run an article on the best way to save the rain forests or *Playgirl* to publish one on how to identify military aircraft. The topic also needs to be meaty enough to give you something to write about without being so complex you can't deal with it in the publication's allotted 500 to 2,500 word count.

The payoff can be practical or it can be sheer fantasy. It makes no difference as long as you identify something a reader really wants to learn or do. Once you've done that, you're half way there.

Form a compelling lead

Lead by showing a reader how happy she'll be once she learns whatever it is that the article's teaching. Do this in a paragraph or two, bringing fiction techniques into play, such as setting a scene using sensory imagery, developing a composite character to play off of or creating a make-believe conversation.

Show her why she needs to know this

Then give her the big picture, for instance, how many women in the country are finding stress relief through nature-related acupuncture. If it's a trend, be sure to mention it and, at the same time, if it's breaking news, say so.

Lay it out...one, two, three

Next spell out, step-by-step, how the reader can achieve whatever it is you're talking about. Make sure you don't sacrifice clarity for cuteness. But don't completely cave in to just the facts. Instead try to make learning painless by writing with a light touch and interjecting your strong voice here and there.

End appropriately

Close by giving her a push to jump in and do it, as if you were handing her a coupon with an expiration date. She needs to participate now, before it's too late. Sometimes you can achieve this sense of urgency by ending with a flourish so inspiring she will have barely put down your article before grabbing the first plane to the Orient, cooking up a batch of French tarts or plunging into water aerobics.

Other times, especially if the subject's complex and the reader could feel a bit overwhelmed, end by laying out the first baby step for her to take.

"I" is Not a Four-Letter Word

WHEN YOU FIRST BEGAN WRITING, chances are you started by putting down what you thought and how you felt. You wrote about the world through the eyes of a first grader.

Then something happened. You graduated to second grade, then third, and your warm, accepting first grade teacher who loved all those wonderful insights that you recorded in block letters and illustrated with the thick Crayola crayons was replaced by the demanding third grade teacher, Miss McNally, who wrote "So what?" in red letters on the side of the paper every time you expressed yourself.

Good writers don't do that, you were told. Wanting to be a good writer, a good anything, you shelved your thoughts and feelings, replacing them with the safe third person point of view, the *he, she, they* point of view from which to tell your stories.

This wasn't all bad, you discovered. In fact, from this vantage point you possessed an Oz-like power to see, hear and think what everyone's doing. Gosh, you were almost God. But being God came with a price, the price of intimacy and connection with the reader. And the worst part was that writing wasn't as much fun anymore.

But a funny thing is happening with feature stories. Writers are sneaking in that first person point of view. Not all writers, mind you. Some of the newer ones, earning their first bylines, still don't dig deep within themselves to find out how they feel about what they're saying. Instead they interview and research then cling tenaciously to their notes as they write their story. Occasionally they'll leave the security of others' thoughts to write a lead, add a transition or two and pen a close. But few dare risk the risen eyebrows of Miss McNally accusing them of inserting their opinion.

A news story about a woman who discovers an environmental hazard in her neighborhood tells just the facts, and that's just what a news story should do. But a feature article should reflect the writer's involvement with the material.

As you read like a feature writer, you'll notice the better, more confident, higher-paid writers do write with a personal point of view toward their material, whether they're writing about a woman or an issue. Sometimes the writer's attitude is blatant, she's there in the first person, but other times it's subtle, with a simple interpretation here or there.

I once heard an editor from *Vanity Fair* say how much he—and editors from other well-written publications—wants the writers in their stories. "The better the writer, the more she's in there," he said. He then went on to say that writers should probe what's special about themselves, the things that make them who they are, and exploit them, instead of thinking "I'm a writer, everything's grist for the mill." By knowing who you are, you make a bridge to the subject and then a bridge to the reader. Take this specialty, develop it and sell it.

Dominick Dunne—whose daughter was strangled by a killer who got off with a measly five years—seems to make a freelance career out of covering some of the most salacious trials of the century, including those of the Menendez brothers and O.J. Simpson.

Southern-reared Rick Bragg, writing for *The New York Times*, earned a Pulitzer Prize for profiling Oseola McCarty, an elderly scrubwoman who donated her life's savings of $150,000 to a local college. Similar to his subject, Rick grew up "dirt poor in Alabama," and knew first hand of the deprivation of which he wrote. This undoubtedly contributed to the sensitivity, sharp detail and insight that he brought to the piece. Later he wrote *All Over But the Shoutin'*, a tribute to his mother, a woman not unlike Oseola.

Writing with an attitude, so to speak, doesn't come easily. Those of us trained in journalism school were taught to avoid the pronoun "I." And many of us didn't fight back. It was easier to let others feed us the information and write on autopilot. But as we grew as writers and as humans, we wanted more. We wanted back what Miss McNally took from us in third grade. We wanted to *really* write.

Today real writing means real risk-taking. We might come out sounding like an egotistical, pompous fool to be avoided, even if we were the last survivors of a nuclear blast.

So let's see how we can write without embarrassing our mothers. Let's begin by acknowledging that what we really want when we write feature stories is to give our reader an experience, whether it's a laugh, a cry or a lesson. We want to move her emotionally, to change her in some small way. OK. So how do we do it? Surely not by giving her a data dump of information. This would do nothing but overwhelm her and/or bore her. Instead we offer the reader a slice of our life in the decisions about what we chose to dramatize, in the quotes we select, in the judgmental transitions we write, in just about everything we put on paper. If we do this timidly, just dipping our toes in the swirling current of a feature article, our reader will be unmoved, unimpressed. We have to bless ourselves and dive head-first.

> 🐝 *First off, get an attitude.*
> *A writer with an attitude towards*
> *her subject naturally writes with*
> *a strong voice.*

First off, get an attitude. A writer with an attitude towards her subject naturally writes with a strong voice. This is what will determine the thrust of your piece.

Find out how you feel about a story or an issue. After you come home from an interview sit down, be very quiet, and ask yourself how you feel—about the woman, the issue, whatever. Are you inspired? Or are you a bit turned off, maybe a whole lot turned off? Do you feel that the subject was leveling with you or should you go back again, and maybe again, to peel off another layer to reach her core?

How you feel about a story is vital information. You're an important part of the story.

Try this: Write a paragraph or two about something that really makes you cringe. This may be something everyone else considers petty, but it bugs you to death. Now read what you wrote. Tell me, does this have a weasel voice? Or are the words wrapped in passion and fueled with emotion? The latter, I'll wager.

Sometimes writers with very strong viewpoints towards their material never use the I-word—even once—and that's fine. Their take is so strong they're already in every word.

A few writers unabashedly write the entire piece in the first person. But even these language hussies seldom use "I" more than a few times. They start off with an "I," but soon the "I" vanishes as they get wrapped up in the story. The "I" may reappear a few paragraphs later and once again at the end. It really doesn't matter. What does matter is that by beginning the story with "I," the writer has reached the reader on a more intimate level than she would have if she stuck to Miss McNally's rule.

I tell corporate writers, who are often forced by constraints beyond their control to never use "I," to use it in their stories and then, when they finish, to go back and edit it out. This will help them retain a strong personal connection with the reader.

A friend, Sue Campbell, who edits the lifestyle section of the *St. Paul Pioneer Press,* shared this first person story with me. As a freelancer for a regional magazine, she wrote about Maryland bird watchers who woke before dawn every Saturday to wade knee-deep in muddy swamps waiting for certain birds to arrive.

Although these aficionados knew the birds' names, migration patterns, mating habits and probably even their fine china choices, they were unable to transfer their enthusiasm to Sue. When she first wrote the story, the bird watchers came across as feather brains.

You know what she had to do? Get up at the crack of dawn, wade knee-deep in the mud with the bird watchers and experience firsthand the exhilaration of the birds' arrival. Now she never claimed to share the group's passion—and swears you'll never find her spending another Saturday morning that way—still there was something about being there that she was able to translate to her readers so they shared the experience.

Another time Sue wrote a story about an octogenarian who was president of the old woodies roller coaster club. Sue's research included riding these old woodies with him. It would be tough for readers to identify with this gentleman, Sue reasoned, so at the very beginning of the story she inserted herself, explaining that she was a newly married freelance writer intrigued by these fans of the old Coney Island style coasters.

We, the readers, became Sue. We hopped in with her as she joined this great-grandfather for the coaster's climb up that first big hill. In the middle of the piece, as Sue and her companion are about to make the death-defying drop, she looks around the amusement park. The view is unobstructed because, as readers, we're sitting in the first seat where her guide has insisted they sit.

The blood drains from Sue's face as the coaster stands, seemingly suspended on top of the track, waiting for the pull of gravity to take over. She looks to her companion for comfort; he's lighting up a cigarette. Finally they reach the bottom and Sue unwraps her fingers, one-by-one, from the cold metal bar.

Meanwhile, we learn the history of these old woodies, the numbers still in existence and their safety record. We might also meet a bride whose groom proposed while riding a woodie. But the thread that draws us through the story is Sue, because Sue's writing in the first person, even if only for three or four sentences, puts us right there in her seat. And how many of us could stop reading when we're perched 150 feet above the midway?

You don't have to wait until you're on top of the world to put yourself in a story. Jeanne Marie Laskas, a contributor to *Good House-keeping*, did so very cleverly when she wrote about visiting a single mom who adopted three special needs kids. Jeanne Marie put us in this unique mom's world by interpreting for us. At one point in the day, the writer told us how tired she was just shadowing this mother as she cared for her brood. Jeanne Marie did not yawn in every paragraph. She was subtle but the reader got the message. Be alert for these simple strategies when you read articles, and emulate them.

The ultimate "I" story has to be one published by *Redbook*. The article was titled "A Day In The Life Of My Penis."

Yes, it was written by a man. Lots of men make it between the covers of the women's magazines and often they're welcomed royally. In fact, one freelancer I know actually masqueraded as a man—not exactly lying, mind you, only using the male derivative of her name—because she believed the field of women's stories was more open to men.

The trick that makes the penis story, or any highly personalized point-of-view piece-work, is to ask if your personal thoughts have universal appeal. The Miss McNallys of the world feel they have to be vigilantes against the everything-I-feel-and-everything-I-think-and-everything-I-do-is-important type of writing. And they are right, this writing belongs in your journal for only your mommy to see.

But there is a midway point between never allowing yourself to surface in a story and tap dancing in the spotlight. Read attentively to see how others find this mid-ground. Think hard about what you want to say about the material, and introduce yourself to the reader, never taking your eyes off her. If you concentrate on what she wants, you'll enjoy a warm and lasting relationship.

Channeling

SOMETIMES WHEN YOU WRITE ABOUT A WOMAN, her story includes a child or even a pet who figures prominently in the narrative. Sometimes, and she may not like this, the child or pet is more important than she is to the story. So you must shift the spotlight of your prose from this bright, articulate woman to a toddler or a terrier who gurgles or growls.

Now this is not to say that these silent types, kids, dogs and the like, are not thinking thoughts worth noting or aren't experiencing powerful feelings. They are. And it's up to you to channel these thoughts and feelings from their mind and heart into the reader's. Sometimes these thoughts and feelings can be "read" by other subjects in the story; other times, you're it.

The ability to channel gives you a tool to find and write stories others overlook because they don't know the power of interpreting what these silent types are thinking and feeling. Channeling's easier than eating lo mein with chop sticks, and the best part is few people do it. This means that your friend, who is always getting published while you're getting rejected—although you're the better writer, even if the editors haven't caught on—will be wondering what's up when you're byline starts appearing more often than a politician's excuses.

Channeling isn't mystical. You do not need great wisdom nor wonderful insights nor a 2,800-year-old spirit named Rah. What you do need is a keen eye to look at something and really see it. One good way to sharpen your observation skills is to enter a railroad station, restaurant, office even a rest-room, give yourself two minutes, then walk out and write down everything you remember seeing. Now go back and look again. What important things did you miss? Another is to commit yourself to record in a notebook daily something you observed. Periodically read your entries. You'll be surprised how your observations have grown more precise, more astute.

Beyond keen observation, a skill needed to channel well is interpretation and here, the password is trust. There's no right or wrong to how you read a nonverbal someone's actions or attitudes. It's your informed, intelligent and caring viewpoint that makes it work. Often this is the toughest part of channeling.

"Who named you pope?" the naysayers inside you heckle. Your views don't need to be heralded by giant puffs of white smoke from the Vatican to be valid. But they do need to be cushioned with the confidence only you can give them.

If you're starting to squirm because this sounds too much like mind-reading or voodoo, and you're thinking, "All I wanted to do was write a story and see my name in print," relax, you will. And you won't have to give up your family, quit your day job or join a cult. Channeling was taught to me by, imagine this, an editor at *Reader's Digest*. No, she didn't label it as such. She was assigning me the story of the dog who found a baby lost in the desert. Her words were: "Describe the search through the dog's eyes. Get the owner to 'read' the dog." If the editors of a magazine as godlike as the *Digest* advocate channeling, can you resist?

"Lost in the Desert" was one of the *Digest's* most widely read dramas. But without channeling, I would have been lucky if my mother had read it. The heroine of the story was a German shepherd named Kallie who rescued a toddler near death. This dog arrived with a checkered history of searching and a phobia for noises. She also had, as we learn at the end of the story, an indomitable spirit that kept her searching despite exhaustion and pain. The point is, Kallie had to come alive for the reader, she had to be unlike any other dog they've known. Channeling made this happen.

Take a look at these interpretive leaps made by Kallie's owner, Nancy:

> "Let's get back to work, girl," Nancy coaxed. The dog cowered, *her confidence shaken.* "Let's go, girl," Nancy repeated. Slowly and cautiously, Kallie began tracking again.
>
> With every passing hour, hopes of finding Derrek alive diminished. Nancy pictured the toddler wandering in the dark, stumbling, calling out to his mother. She removed Derrek's sock from her backpack and put it close to Kallie's nose. "Check it out, Kallie. Is this Derrek?" The dog's eyes met hers as if to say, *"I'm doing my best."* She stroked the animal's coat. If Kallie sensed her handler doubted her, the dog's confidence would fade completely.

...Suddenly, Kallie began to yip in pain. Cactus spines had pierced the padding on her paws.

"Roll over," Nancy ordered. She removed a pair of surgical pliers for just such an emergency from her backpack and pulled out a dozen spines. Kallie's paw puffed immediately. *"I'm not budging,"* she seemed to say.

"Come on, girl, let's work," Nancy coached. Kallie rose slowly, determined to please her mistress.

...Exhausted, her paws sore and swollen, Kallie *strained to keep going.* How much longer can she push herself? Nancy wondered.

Then an astonishing thing happened. *As if propelled by an unseen force*, Kallie raised her nose into the air and began to track furiously.

...A couple of feet away stood Kallie, her tail wagging furiously. *"Did I do good?"* she seemed to ask. Nancy patted the dog and gave her a sip of water too.

We have Nancy vouching for such feelings as her dog's confidence being shaken. Later she explains that Kallie's eyes met hers as if to say, "I'm doing my best." Still another time Kallie is credited with seeming to say "I'm not budging." With her "paws sore and swollen" she "strained to keep going."

And, are you ready for this one? Through channeling, we learn that Kallie enjoys a spiritual experience, "an astonishing thing happened. As if propelled by an unseen force, Kallie raised her nose into the air and began to track furiously."

OK. You want to channel the next kid or black cat who crosses your path. You've even threatened to channel your partner if he doesn't start speaking. You know that to channel someone's thoughts or feelings you must observe them and then give meaning to what you see. But exactly how do you do this?

Forget crystal balls, burning incense or heavy dark velvet draperies. All you need is a pad and pen and a willingness to quiet yourself, open your mind and be confident to trust what the voice deep within has to say.

Early on, I asked Nancy for a thumbnail sketch of the story—a toddler lost in the Arizona desert for four days and rescued just in time—and I drew a time line of important moments of the search. Then I asked her to walk me through the drama, one paw step at a time, from the moment her pager went off alerting her to the missing child, to the reunion she and her dog had with the toddler a year after the rescue. I stopped her often to ask, "What was Kallie doing then? How do you think she felt? Why? What did you notice that made you think that?"

As the drama intensified, so did my questions. I asked anything and everything. Especially stupid questions. The stupid questions sometimes produced the best stuff, leading Nancy in directions I'd never know to ask about if I'd thought only laterally.

Nancy was a natural at reading Kallie. Ask any new mother who's smitten with her baby what their goo-goos and gaggles mean and she'll tell you more than you want to hear. But if you run across a subject who's a klutz at playing the game, make your own leaps of interpretation, then check them out with her.

Consider a few passages from a trilogy of amazing animal profiles for *McCall's*. Animals, once thought to be dumb, are anything but. In fact, these three are downright extraordinary. But without channeling the feelings and the motivations of these furry heroes, their stories would be nothing more than journal entries.

Here's a moment from a story about Flopsy, a rabbit who visits children at the Shriner's Burn Institute. Animal therapist Ginny Cornett finds the one spot on a severely burned little girl that's not bandaged.

> She lightly brushed the child's foot once across the rabbit's soft fur. Meghan froze. Flopsy looked up as *if to ask, "What's happening?"*
>
> Ginny waited, then swept Meghan's foot again. This time Meghan seemed to breath out. And Ginny could almost see a look of wonder beneath those bandages. *Flopsy's eyes, too, brightened.*
>
> "Flopsy enjoys an uncanny ability to read patients," Ginny says. *"If someone's depressed, she nuzzles up to them. If they're energetic, she feeds their mood."*
>
> ...When kids get a bit wild, she turns to Ginny seemingly to say, *"Hey, get me out of here."*
>
> ...Sharing the spotlight with fashion designer Carolina Herrera, Crown Princess Marie-Chantal of Greece and Nancy Kissinger made little impression on the rabbit. Instead *she longingly eyed* the floral centerpieces brimming with fresh greenery.

This second profile spotlights Ringo, the 26-pound red tabby Manx, who saved his family from a toxic methane leak under their house that could have exploded and claimed their lives.

...From a running start at the end of the hall, he flung himself against the front door. Carol couldn't imagine what he wanted. He did it again and again. Carol opened the door, but Ringo just stood there. "I could have bopped him," she said. Then Ringo meowed and caught Carol's eye and her annoyance turned to concern. *"It was as if he were pleading with me,"* she recalls.

Carol had seen that look before. Three years ago she found Ringo with his mother and litter mates in an old shed struggling to survive. Carol already had three cats and didn't want another, but then *Ringo looked straight into her eyes.*

Now, on this late August day, *he was trying again to reach her.*

"What's your problem, boy?" she asked.

Ringo turned over on his back with his paws pointing to the ceiling.

"Want me to come out?" Carol asked, scrambling for answers.

Hearing those words Ringo *jumped up and tilted his ears forward as if to say "finally."*

Carol followed him out the front door. He took a few steps, then waited for her to catch up. He led her 60 feet from the house to an area of the yard where they seldom went.

...As Carol watched intently, Ringo dug so vigorously in the hard lava landscaping surrounding the meter she was sure the soft pads of his paws would bleed. "Then *suddenly he stopped, opened his mouth, curled his lips and pulled his nose up to tell me something smelled,"* she says.

Third, the story of Bruno, the country's only dog working as both a guide and service dog—providing the eyes and limbs for Natalie Wormeli, a young attorney who is blind and a wheelchair user.

Bruno earned her confidence again the day they were in the middle of the street and an ambulance roared up from behind, its sirens blaring. *"Bruno was unflap-pable,"* she says. *"You could sense he was thinking."*

Another thing to think about when you're channeling animals, is to avoid reducing them to little people in fur coats. Watch what they do and how they react. Study their expressions. Learn their histories, their likes, dislikes, their eccentricities. What makes this cat, rabbit or rat different from every other? Be open to your perceptions, hunches and intuition. Then check these with their owner, trainer or anyone who loves them.

By now you know everything you need to channel pets, so let's move on to the human variety, kids, for instance.

"Fuzzy Bear and Jason; A Very Special Friendship," published by *Family Circle,* was nominated for the Dog Writers' of America Association award for feature writing. It, too, would have been a dog of a story, so to speak, if I hadn't channeled.

Here's the plot. Nine-year-old Jason Hunter stopped speaking when his beloved dog Fuzzy Bear died. The child, who has Down syndrome and multiple handicaps, remained silent for six months until a New-foundland puppy named Two Bear became his pet. Like Jason, Two Bear also has special needs, and because of their disabilities the two forged an unusual bond based on helping one another.

When I queried the editor, I told the story through Jason's mother's eyes. I had spoken with Debbie Hunter twice on the phone, so it seemed hers would be the natural viewpoint to take.

The editor didn't agree.

"Tell it from the child's point of view," she said.

"Sure."

Three-thousand words gleaned from the mouth of a little boy with Down syndrome and other disabilities, who never formed sentences longer than five words. This would be a tough assignment from *any* child's point of view. When kids said the darndest things to Art Linkletter, they only said a few lines—not a whole story.

Did I tell the editor this?

Not exactly.

What did I say?

How about, "Great idea."

So here I was with this "great idea" and no hint of how to pull it off. (I'll bet the editor didn't have a clue either.)

A few days later I was riding on a train from Richmond, Virginia, when I overheard two women who were sitting in front of me praising an autobiography written by an autistic woman named Donna Williams. They said the book *Nobody Nowhere* provided the reader with a glimpse into a world previously known only to autistics.

My interest soared. Their words made me a card-carrying proponent of serendipity. (This was before the *Digest* editor mentioned channeling, so I needed all the celestial intervention I could get.) Something inside me stirred when I heard those women speak about that book. I sensed it would help me describe Jason's inner world.

If you're befuddled, so am I. Serendipity is like that. Dictionaries define it as the faculty for making fortunate discoveries by accident. It's kind of like lining up your armies for battle. Serendipity is the wise brave general. Having him on your side doesn't mean you can raise the victory flag just yet. But it's unfurled at the bottom of the pole, and the troops are smiling.

And while I know you can't order serendipity like a garlic bagel warm with salmon, lettuce, tomato, red onion and alfalfa sprouts, you can strongly encourage it. How? Start by saying aloud what you need to make your story work. Then, like a baby bird with his mouth open wide, be receptive to being fed what you need by some mysterious force of the universe. That's it. It works. And you don't pay taxes on what comes your way.

When I reached Maryland, I hurried off the train and straight to Super Crown books. There on the shelf, just as I had imagined, was a copy of the book. By the end of page 3, I was sold. It showed me—in a circuitous way that maybe no one else would have understood—how to know what Jason was thinking and feeling, when he didn't say a word. And, most important, how to feed this to the reader.

Here are a few passages from the story. Each shows how Jason's life is decoded by his mother, brother or the writer.

> At school he had been introduced to sign language, and, when his sign instructor left, Debi had an idea: She would continue to teach Jason to sign. She bought an instruction book, and as Jason would sign a word, she'd speak it. Soon Jason's small hands were dancing across his chest, forming large expressive signs, *his face glowing with the happy thoughts and pouting with the sad ones.* "He was turning into a real ham," his brother Larry recalls.
>
> Gradually Jason began to replace his repertoire of 350 signs with speech, building up to four and five-word

sentences: "Give me juice, Mom, please." His family was thrilled. With each new word, new phrase and new thought, Jason's life became richer and fuller.

Then came the day when Fuzzy Bear had to be "put to sleep." Unable to comprehend what really happened, Jason found his window on the world suddenly slammed shut when he realized his beloved pet was gone. "Where's Fuzzy Bear?" Jason signed, as he watched his mother pack away the dog's big yellow dish. His pudgy index finger was waving wildly. Debi was taken aback, she had tried to prepare him for this day. "Fuzzy Bear was very old and sick and she's in heaven now," Debi whispered. As she spoke, *she wondered if any child, especially one like Jason, could really understand what happened.* Sitting cross-legged on the floor, she pulled him close and cradled his body. "Fuzzy Bear won't be coming home, but she'll always love you."

Jason's eyes filled with tears as he hugged his mother with all his might. "Fuzzy Bear loved me," he said. Then he fell silent. On April 29, 1992, *Jason lost more than his voice; he lost contact with the world* his family had struggled to create.

Jason no longer begged his brothers to play, and when they tried to engage him with his favorite toy, Popeye, he grew even more distant. He slouched around the house, head low, eyes downcast. He awoke during the night crying from nightmares. He'd spend hours alone in his room listening to music. *"Overnight he changed from a 6-year-old to an old man,"* his brother Larry recalls.

"...Maybe he blamed us for taking his dog away," Debi says now. Whenever she knelt to hug Jason, *his eyes, strained, darted up and down and side to side, never meeting hers.* "Say something, anything," she'd beg him. "I thought I was going to lose my mind," she admits. "I needed to hear him say, 'I love you, Mommy.'"

"See what we brought home," Debi called to Jason from the foot of the stairs one chilly November afternoon. When Jason spotted the bundle of grayish-black fur wiggling in her arms, his face lit up. Propelled by sheer determination, Jason's weak legs carried him down the 18 steps from their apartment to grab the puppy from her.

Although surprised by Jason's enthusiasm, nothing could have prepared her for what occurred next. "Fuzzy Bear's baby?" the little boy asked, his voice strong, distinct.

"The transformation in Jason seemed nothing short of a miracle. *The child's personality and health blossomed*," says his pediatrician, Robert Morton, M.D. Two Bears' influence was evident in school too. "His whole face brightened when we mentioned her."

When you look closer at these interpretations you see that some are derived from visual clues like "his face glowing with the happy thoughts and pouting with the sad ones" or "his eyes strained, darted up and down, and side to side never meeting hers." Others stem from Debi's view of Jason, "she wondered if any child, especially one like Jason, could really understand what happened." Still others are based on opinion, like this one made by Jason's older brother, "Overnight he changed from a 6-year-old to an old man," his doctor opines. "The child's personality and health blossomed."

I even took it upon myself to write, "Jason lost more than his voice; he lost contact with the world...." But before I could do this I had to wrestle to the ground the voices in my head asking in a very indignant tone, "Who do you think you are? A columnist or something?"

"Haven't I worked hard enough?" I pleaded. (These voices never listen to reason.) "Look my coffee's cold and yesterday's uneaten lunch is still on my desk."

"So what?" they sneered. Then they got rough, accusing me of being a fraud. "Four weeks ago you didn't even know a Jason," they shouted, throwing rationality back in my face.

These inner critics are toddlers who, when they don't get their way, fall to the floor in the middle of the supermarket aisle, pound their fists and scream at the top of their lungs that they hate you. Finally, they hold their breath, turn red, even pass out. You've got no choice. Quiet them however you can—by reason or violence.

With interpretations you give the reader a hand—or is it a paw? And the reader often discovers those who don't speak a word may have the most to say.

My Unlicensed Shrink

IN ONE OF MY LAST GRADUATE SCHOOL CLASSES at Hopkins the professor not only analyzed my paper, he analyzed me. It was the most revealing lesson I've ever learned in a writing class. And naturally it was painful.

Here's how it happened. First the instructor critiqued a story I wrote about a mother who spent 25 years searching for a daughter taken from her arms as an infant. Here is my lead:

> On a summer afternoon in 1969, 6-year-old Melease McClain was rummaging through her grandmother's cedar chest when she spotted a birth certificate embossed with a gold seal. Intrigued, the first grader began sounding out the words on the parchment: Vicky Irene McClain.
>
> "Who is this?" Melease asked, running to her mother. Holding her daughter tight, Barbara McClain, then 21, began to cry. "She's your little sister," she said. "She was taken from us long ago," but she'll be home someday."

So far, OK. But a few paragraphs later, I committed a felony, a data dump.

> "From that moment, I lost my childhood," recalls Melease, now 31 and married, with four children of her own. She and her mother began a passionate 23-year search to find her sister, a search that pitted them against a state bureaucracy that stonewalled them at every turn.
>
> It was a spring afternoon in 1965 that a solemn-faced state social worker from the Lake County Courthouse in Tiptonville, Tennessee, knocked on the door of Barbara McClain's one-bedroom wood-frame house in

the small town of Ridgely. Barbara stood listening in horror as the woman explained that Barbara's own father, Neely Gray, had summoned her to take Barbara's daughters: 2-year-old Melease and 6-week-old Vicky. She told Barbara the children were too great a burden for a young woman who was still a minor and whose husband provided little support.

Barbara had married Charles McClain, a 19-year-old cotton picker, soon after she turned 14. Three months later she was expecting Melease and her husband had gone off to work odd jobs, something he would do throughout their marriage. He seldom sent money home to his wife.

According to Barbara, her father disapproved of her husband and hoped that if the children were out of the picture, Charles McClain would disappear as well. Although Barbara was living rent-free in a friend's home and receiving the same packages of surplus government food that were provided to many families in their poor rural town, her father was worried that someday her children might become his responsibility.

"It reads like it's on a spring," the instructor chided. "Too dense, too tightly woven, too much for the reader to swallow. This is not a homework assignment. Seduce the reader. Slowly suck her in."

Fine. I saw my mistakes. You can stop now, I thought. But he didn't.

"A lead like yours shows the insecurity of the writer," he said, softly. No matter how softly he spoke, I still felt exposed, naked in front of 18 classmates who dared not to look.

Sure I'm insecure, I thought. What writer isn't? And this is going to help?

"Screw the reader," he lambasted.

"Hold on," I thought to myself. "Hadn't we spent a semester trying to connect with the reader?" But before I could find my voice, still buried in embarrassment, he went on.

"Be confident. If the reader's not willing to stay with you, to hell with her," he said. "What this lead shows is that you are not sure enough of your ability to tell the story, so you try to cram everything in the first few paragraphs."

Well, hang me for that one.

I looked around, trying to act casual. Everyone was looking everywhere but at me. Their kindness made be feel sicker. Of course I'd be kind too, if he were dissecting one of them.

And the worse part was, he was absolutely right.

Then he flipped to a second story, this one about 12-year-old Richie who was killed while riding his bike to school. "She's got a real ear for the spoken word," he said.

> "Someday I'll be face-to-face with God and he'd better have a good explanation for why both my children had to die," Sandy said. "But then it won't matter, because I'll be with my boys again."

Hmmm. At last I did something right, I thought to myself.

Not a chance.

"But look," he continued. "The writer is so unsure of herself that she's afraid you won't be there at the end so she puts this quote up high, where it doesn't belong. It should close the story," he said. "But again the writer...."

For God's sakes, say my name, I thought. What do I have to lose at this point? Privacy? Self-respect? Pride? They took leave with the lead.

If I didn't respect him so—he was well-published—I could have dismissed him. But the truth was, he was reading me too well.

"Confidence," he continued. "Confidence is what it comes down to. You've got to believe that what you have to say is valuable to the reader and that you will be captivating enough to carry her along for the whole ride. And if she doesn't stay for the journey, to hell with her."

Confidence. Confidence. Confidence.

When's this ever going to end? I wondered.

Then he went for the artery, ordering the group to "consider these paragraphs":

> Barbara began crisscrossing Tennessee searching courthouse records, welfare offices and sheriff's departments for any trace of her daughter. She'd sleep in her car, and often she'd skip meals to finance trips. Sometimes she took her children with her; at other times her sister would care for them. "How could they take my baby away?" she asked officials wherever she went. "I was never given any papers to sign. I was never told to go to court."

> When Melease was 6, Barbara and Charles McClain
> divorced. Later, she married Ed Bridges, a devoted fam-
> ily man with whom she had two more sons. Tragically,
> he was killed in a diving accident in 1973.

Whew. I thought to myself. At last he's found something good to say. The fool I was.

"Again this is a listing that tells the reader too much, it overwhelms her. What the writer...."

Here we go again with "the writer."

"What the writer should have done is to select one or two of these items and show what they mean—not tell about them. This is too much to comprehend. She then could have narrated, or talked us through, a few of the points she didn't dramatize."

OK. Let's end it on neutral ground. Nonthreatening.

"Take a look at this list," he continued, back to the story about 12-year-old Richie.

> A straight-A student, Richie had just been elected
> to the student government, started a paper route near
> his home in BePere, Wisconsin and recently confided that
> he received his first kiss.

"What's wrong with it?" he asked the group.

No one said a word.

Hah. For a moment I felt vindicated.

"This is a grouping of unrelated items," he said. "It's jarring to pair getting A's with your first kiss. Group like items together."

Ouch.

These lessons, painful as I found them, come to me every time I put my fingers to the keyboard to write a word. How do I feel about it now? I'll trade a little ego for better writing any day.

The Bye Lines

Fact Checkers

WHEN YOU FINISH INTERVIEWING SOMEONE for a large circulation publication, you'll want to alert her that a fact checker may call.

"A fat checker?" one woman asked, astonished.

"Not a fat checker, a fact checker," I enunciated more clearly.

A fact checker is an employee of the publication whose sole job it is to uncover where you've goofed. With the tenaciousness of a terrier, she'll retrace your every step in researching and writing, looking for a slip, a bump or a downright fall-flat-on-your-face foul-up.

Every publication sets its own standard for accuracy in the words they print. *Reader's Digest*, for example, prides itself on observing one of the highest. Occasionally *Digest* editors mention the stories you'll never read in their magazine because they were too good to be true, literally.

I recall one *Digest* checker who was dogged in her pursuit of the truth. In "Lost In the Desert" I wrote:

> As the youngest of five daughters, Nancy had enjoyed endless hours with her dad when she was growing up. But on June 11, 1979, he was flying a DC-3 that crashed into a remote river. The bodies of the copilot and five passengers surfaced the first week, but her father's corpse could not be located. Nancy agonized over his fate for 33 days until rafters finally discovered his remains. Vowing to try to spare others such pain, she decided to become a search-and-rescue volunteer.

When the checker asked what proof I had of the cause of death, I thought to myself, "Who would ever make up such a story?" But that was beside the point. The checker's job is to confirm, beyond a doubt, what we say to be true.

"No problem," she said cheerfully when I told her I never saw documentation. "I'll track it."

And she did, indeed. First she dug up news articles of the plane crash, then she got a copy of the actual death notice.

Next hitch. When Nancy was unable to recall the exact moment she decided to volunteer, the sentence "vowing to try to spare others such pain, she decided to become a search-and-rescue volunteer" was down graded by the checker to read, "vowing to try to spare others such pain, she *began to think about* becoming a search-and-rescue volunteer." Notice the subtle difference?

Before you pull out your lashes in frustration, let me say that not all fact checkers are this nitpicky. Seems to me that every large publication has its own particular fact-checking personality. (Small publications, incidentally, often rely only on the editor to detect details that may be in error.)

My experience with *McCall's* checkers proves them to be bare bones, just the facts ma'am. They look for correct names, spellings, numbers, oddities that seem to jump out. For instance, they questioned when I said that an animal-assisted therapist took hedgehogs to visit burn patients. (Yes, she did.) Their process seems clean.

Family Circle fact-checking was also sane. A checker there read the subject of a story the gist of her words—not her words verbatim. This to me is cause to throw roses at the checker's feet.

Let me tell you what happens when checkers don't know when to stop talking. Interviewing well is more than asking the right questions; it's creating an ambiance in which your subject feels accepted and safe. One that allows you to chip away at the facade in front of her. And if you're patient and kind (and a little lucky), you earn her trust and are rewarded with honesty. You come away from the interview knowing her.

Then weeks, sometimes months, later, your subject gets a call at 9 a.m. on a Monday morning from a professional sounding voice with a New York accent. This voice proceeds to read back her words. Words that you lovingly collected over tea now seem too invasive, too personal, too revealing. The words read out of context of the story sound brusque, maybe even crude. Your subject protests, insists she never said such a thing, or certainly didn't mean it or meant it only for your ears. Of course you know better and so does the checker.

She tells the checker she wants those quotes deleted. She reneges on your deal. And who wouldn't, considering the circumstances.

A slightly skewed version of this happened to me at one of the Seven Sister magazines when a checker read a mother her own quotes, and those of her grown daughter. The daughter, who is a wife, mother and public relations writer herself, vividly described how her dad's death led to her divorce. The mother wanted the daughter's quotes deleted. I understood this mother's wish to protect her daughter, but this mom needed a tap on the wrist to remind her that her daughter, now a woman, had a right to speak without being edited by her mother.

Surprisingly, the magazine complied with the mother's request. But when the editor phoned soon after, asking me to "up the emotional quotient of the piece to make it more poignant," I saw blood: the editor's. What she wanted was precisely what her checker relinquished all too quickly. And I told her.

I complained that this woman should not have been read her daughter's quotes, and I complained that when the mother objected, the fact-checker and editor gave in rather than giving me a chance to explain to this woman the importance of her daughter's words. I suspect I was not a victim of the magazine's policy as much as a particular personality.

You ask why our conversations weren't taped? They were, and somewhere in the hours of this interview lay the proof of these very revealing sentiments. This mother was not disputing that her daughter said such a thing, she was simply asking—in a very sweet, charming tone—that it not be used. Editors are often mothers too. And when a story is emotionally driven, as this one was—and contains a tinge of celebrity—they have been known to acquiesce to a subject's request.

So take a deep breath. All's not lost. You can learn to work within the system of checks. Maybe it's a stretch to say you can tame a feral fact checker into a friend, but she certainly can become a partner. After all, you both want the same thing, an error-free story.

Here are eight simple strategies that will help:

• From the germ of a story idea start a file. An accordion type in which you can pitch everything related to the piece works well. Notice I didn't say to file your paperwork, just pitch it. Sure it's nice to be the type of writer who rewrites notes, alphabetizes phone numbers and does myriad other prissy little acts. But that's just it, it's nice. It doesn't make you a better writer, simply a better-organized writer.

• Keep your notes legible. At the beginning of each interview, ask your subject to spell her whole name, no matter how simple it seems. Verify addresses, work and home phone numbers, and put all this information at the top of your notebook. Checkers get very testy if they can't reach someone when they want, and there's nothing you want less than a testy checker.

• Tape all important interviews, in person and over the phone. Then take notes too, big broad notes with main ideas and general impressions. Always ask permission to tape, then be casual about it, and your subject will be too.

• Go to original sources on any controversial matters. Examples are court records, police records and other government documents. Keep copies of all of these in your file. Try for two, three, even four collaborations on any potentially libelous material.

Buy a good book on the writer and the law, and learn all you can through writers' groups such as The American Society of Journalists and Authors (ASJA), based in Manhattan. With or without checkers, all publications place the onus for accuracy squarely on the writer. Some even ask us to sign contracts saying we'll reimburse the publication for legal fees required to defend themselves in court if we are found wrong. Whew. Bring on those nitpicky fact checkers.

• Create a paper trail of newspaper articles, court documents, journals, diaries, tax statements, letters, Day-timers, anything to prove the veracity of what you write. Any type of paper trail helps.

• If you suspect your subject may be skittish about something you're writing, broach this with her before you submit your story. Here you want to be careful not to stir up new concerns. But if you think she might waffle on the facts when a checker phones, it's better for you to uncover and deal with the concerns yourself.

Occasionally, a savvy editor can intercede and soothe raw nerves between writer and her subject on a delicate point. When I wrote about a young woman who was sexually abused as a child by her mother's boyfriend, I wanted to verify a few points involving the Big Sisters organization. Their representatives told me it would be easier to simply fax them the copy and they'd locate the principals involved and get back to me. It was the start of a holiday weekend and my deadline was fast approaching so I complied. Big mistake. They showed the story to the young woman who had been abused and when she read about her childhood trauma she panicked. She told Big Sisters she didn't want it in the story and they felt a special need to protect one of their former Little Sisters. Of course she knew from the beginning that this was the story. Her words were taped and on the record. Fortunately, a very smart and soothing editor from *Family Circle* held her hand over the phone for a few minutes and all was well. She needed the reassurance from a third party that she would not come across poorly to readers. Still it's far better to head off such showdowns.

• With the larger periodicals, once your article is accepted, you'll be asked to mail in your material. This means everything, including background stuff such as books, articles, notes, even tangential interviews—everything anyone uttered about the story that influenced you.

Remember, before you send it—by certified, return receipt requested, mail for obvious reasons—look it over again. This can be painful. By now you're sick of the piece. So why do it? Call it story preservation, if you like.

When the fact checker phones, be sure you sound intelligent, confident, in control. If you haven't looked at your notes for weeks, are immersed up to your split ends in another story and your mother-in-law has just dropped by for a short chat about your housekeeping skills, you can find a question such as, "what's her husband's name?" to be downright mystifying. You begin running through the alphabet and reach only the Cs, when the fact checker sarcastically snaps, "Never mind, I thought you could handle it, I'll find it myself."

Sounding befuddled chills the checker. It's an embossed invitation for a shark attack. She's nervous. Her job's on the line. If errors make it into print, she's fetching coffee full-time.

• The checker is a human being. She's got a sassy teen, a pesky neighbor and a dog that barks all night. Be the first writer to be courteous, and chances are she'll be rooting for you and your story. Believe it or not, there's nothing a fact checker wants more than to send your story back up to the editor with the words scrawled across the top: "Perfect. Ready to print."

To Market

FINDING A HOME FOR A WOMAN'S STORY is like going to lunch with someone new. First you try to find out what interests her. Then you quickly size up whether she's the type for cocktail party chatter or a thoughtful discussion. You attempt to inhabit her head. What stresses her? What inspires her? You try to avoid topics that irritate her.

Just as each woman has her own personality, each newspaper or magazine has its own voice. Tailor what you write to that voice. Do the coverlines and articles reveal a trace of humor? Sex? Warmth? Family values? The better you know the publication, the better chance you will have to write for it.

A good way to get inside information about a magazine's needs and wants is to read its writer's guidelines. A magazine's guidelines are written by its editors for writers who wish to write for them. The best guidelines spell out exactly what editors are looking for, including which features or columns are open to freelancers, subject matter, tone, voice and word count. Often they list how much they will pay. Send the magazines a self-addressed, stamped envelope and a note requesting the guidelines or look the guidelines up in *The American Directory of Writer's Guidelines* available at libraries and bookstores.

Women's magazines change editorial content because the reader herself changes. Trends come, trends go. Magazines continually survey their readers to determine what's happening and what's important in their lives.

And, if by chance, the reader doesn't change, the editor does. It's a revolving door at the Seven Sisters magazines. One editor quipped that the most she could hope for was to die before she passed through the seventh.

If you think *Redbook, Allure* or *Self* are the same as three years ago, or even last year, look again. This goes for any woman's magazine or newspaper's lifestyle section. To the casual reader, the shift in content, tone or attitude is undefinable. But to you, a writer who scrutinizes each issue like it's your charge account, a baby step in any direction shouts opportunity. Any movement, one way or another, opens pockets waiting to be filled with words from you.

One constant you can count on is readers are busier than ever. They want to learn how to manage stress, boost their energy and do things better and faster. Another is that nearly every woman wants to improve her relationships—relationships with everyone from her partner, to her sister-in-law, to the crotchety neighbor next door, to the person who grooms her dog.

Consider also that stories are getting shorter and punchier for today's time-starved readers, but their messages are just as strong. *Mademoiselle* solves one of life's biggest problems on one page: "Should You Marry Him?"

❦ ❦ ❦

Here are 39 things editors like in the writers they work with and the women's stories they buy.

• Editors like writers who can spot an issue that's coming up and focus it so readers can identify with feelings they cannot yet articulate.
• Editors like writers who propose a fresh idea that tells them something they didn't know and explain why it's important to the reader.
• Editors like writers who reveal in a query a few questions they'll ask a subject and then promise even more.
• Editors like writers who write from their own experience, providing added dimension to the story idea.
• Editors like writers who make the universe personal.
New Woman published a first person story by a woman who had ambivalent feelings about her abortion. This took a polarized political debate and made it human.
• Editors like writers who craft stories with emotional honesty.
New Woman featured a woman who told with brutal honesty what it was like growing up with a mother so young that they reared one another.
• Editors like writers who pique their curiosity because they know they'll do the same with the reader.
When the writer who had the idea to write about women entering the convent to become nuns after they've lived full lives queried the editor about it, the editor was intrigued to know why a woman who

has been out in the world would choose a cloistered life. She was certain her readers would want to know too, so she assigned the story.

• Editors like writers who don't give everything in the story equal weight.

Some points are probed deeply, while others are glazed over.

• Editors like writers who create provocative, not gimmicky, queries.

• Editors want stories that are touching, not tabloid.

• Editors like writers who bring them stories with that one powerful detail that makes them gasp and say, "Oh my God, I can't believe it."

• Editors like stories that give readers an emotional payoff—even if the ending isn't happy.

• Editors like stories that inspire readers.

• Editors like stories that deal with spirituality—subtly.

The largest selling issues of *Time* and *Newsweek* had angels on their covers.

• Editors like articles that are intensely personal.

If you want to write about your own experience, are you willing to reveal the whole truth about yourself? If not, forget it.

• Editors like stories that deal with a woman's attitude towards money and help her to get a grip on it.

• Editors like stories that take off with a burst of energy, sustain themselves with emotion, and end with something extra that involves the reader.

The story may compel her to pick up her phone and volunteer at the local literacy council or it may leave her with a feeling she carries with her all day.

• Editors like stories with a strong sense of connection to a reader; a news peg is less important.

• Editors like writers whose material has attitude.

• Editors like writers who can tell them their story idea in two sentences.

• Editors like writers who realize feature articles should not have the objectivity of news stories.

Feature articles are written with a strong point of view towards the subject. The idea is shaped, strongly focused and goes somewhere.

• Editors like catchy titles.

Instead of writing "Team Works on CPR," try "Kids Who Save Lives."

• Editors like writers who query with one, two, even three fleshed-out ideas all at once but who do not send a laundry list of suggestions.

• Editors like writers with packaging savvy.

Writers who envision and present a story idea as a published article complete with a coverline, a title, a blurb hyping the piece, a juicy sidebar and photos.

• Editors like writers who time their queries six to eight months ahead for national magazines and three to four months ahead for regional ones.

• Editors like well researched stories that read like it all came trickling out of the writer's mind.

• Editors like stories that are more than just interesting, stories that affect readers' lives.

• Editors like stories that motivate readers to act because readers don't want to just read about other women changing the world or a neighborhood—they want to learn how they can too.

• Editors like stories that present a fresh interpretation of ideas, where the edge meets the midstream.

• Editors like stories about women who will allow their real names to be published, their photos to be taken and who will agree to not speak to other journalists beyond their local press until their story hits the newsstands.

• Editors like current stories.

While there's no specific time when an idea needs to be put to rest, after about two years its complexion starts to fade.

• Editors like relationships with writers, not one night stands.

Target your query to a specific editor at a specific publication. Then, win or loose, target them with another.

• Editors like writers who have a brain full of insights and write insightful prose.

• Editors like writers who put themselves out on the edge with honesty.

• Editors like writers who collaborate well with them.

A hint: When an editor says "We might want to leave out your interview with the gynecologist," delete the *might*, and you've got the gist of the sentence. She's trying to be politic; she's really not open to negotiation. If something's super important to you, then explain your point. But as your mother always said, pick your battles.

• Editors like writers who piece together a portrait of their publication's reader.

A *Ladies Home Journal* editor showed how to do this by analyzing coverlines. Holding up a cover from a June issue, she read the theme,

"Have Your Best Summer Ever." Then she read the first coverline, "Bathing Suit Diet, Lose 5 Pounds Fast." This tells you the *Journal* reader, like most of us, needs to lose a few pounds.

The next coverline, "How To Make Time For Yourself," tells you that the reader is probably married and makes time for her husband, her kids, maybe even her aging parents. But she doesn't know how to make time for herself.

"Easy Recipes For Great Get-Togethers" reveals that she likes to cook, otherwise we wouldn't be talking recipes. But notice the term "get-togethers"—we're not speaking of dinner parties.

"Age-Cheater's Little Fixers" hints that she's worrying a little about getting older. She wants to do something about those fine lines starting to appear, but she's not interested in plastic surgery.

"Pesticides and Your Child," it's summer, she's a mom, and she's concerned about poison on her lawn and shrubs.

"Cybil Shepherd and Her Daughter," the reader likes celebrities , especially a celebrity who is a mother.

"Awake at 3 a.m. and Still Can't Get To Sleep," the poor reader has a lot on her mind and she can't settle down.

Put this together and you see a wife and mother who cares about her family and friends and is happy but a little stressed. She wants you, the writer, to help her manage her busy life.

• Editors like writers—with whom they enjoy a relationship—to ask what type of articles they're looking for.

Ask editors for their upcoming themes.

• Editors like writers with whom they've never worked to send a letter explaining what type of stories they want to write, a short bio and clips of published articles.

• Editors like to welcome writers in through the back door of their publication.

One way is to suggest stories appropriate for the regional section of a magazine or a local edition of a big-city newspaper. Another is to hone your skills on a local paper first, following the steps of Erma Bombeck who, in the beginning, gave her words away to a freebie shopper.

Enticing Entitling

IT'S NOT UNLIKELY THAT YOUR TITLE, no matter how long you worked on it or how brilliant it is, will be changed by an editor. Some people say editors change titles just to justify their being on the publisher's payroll. But I'd never say that.

The key is to not become attached to a title. Does this mean you don't have to worry about thinking up a great title? No, of course not. Even if it gets changed later, a great title may be what sells the editor on the project. And who knows? It might even be used.

In general, strive for short, snappy, attention-getting titles that encapsulate the story in a few punchy words.

Scan back issues of the publication you're targeting, absorbing how the titles relate to the actual stories. Notice what tone the titles take, are they light or serious? Try for a title that emulates those used in the publication.

If your title's creative but cryptic, include a subtitle that makes clear exactly what the story's about. Try words like *you, new, latest, health, happiness, quiz, sex* or any superlatives—*greatest, fastest, thinnest, smartest, best.* Or include a number such as "13 Ways to Motivate Your Kids to Earn A's."

Coverlines are important too. You might want to include one or two catchy coverlines when you write your query letter.

You'll notice the coverline often promises more than the story delivers. This is just a little dishonest, so go ahead and do it, make up coverlines that are enticing enough to grab a casual observer's attention as she's strolling past a newsstand.

For instance, a recent cover of *McCall's* shouts, "Stay Safe! The 5 Most Dangerous Places for Women (They're Not What You Think)." This coverline works because it's frightening—"The Most Dangerous Places"—but reassuring, implying that you *will* be safe if you read this article. It's also intriguing: "They're Not What You Think." When you open the magazine, you discover that the main article "What Criminals Don't Want You to Know" is an informative plan for protecting yourself, beginning with trusting your gut. There's also a first person sidebar written by a woman who "refused to be a victim."

❦ If your title's creative but cryptic, include a subtitle that makes clear exactly what the story's about.

Where are the five most dangerous places for women? Boxed on the bottom of the page is the listing: at home, at work, in parking lots and garages, on the road, on jogging and bike paths. Any surprises here? None that I can tell. But that coverline certainly implied so.

Take another example. *Ladies' Home Journal*'s coverline announced the "Secrets of Women Who Look Years Younger." Inside were the winners of the *Journal* and Oil of Olay's "Why I Never Looked Better Contest." Their advice ranged from keeping your hair short to moisturizing your skin, to getting plenty of exercise, to staying informed. All good suggestions. But secrets? Hardly.

The Numbers Game

I SUPPOSE YOU'VE ALREADY GUESSED my dirty little secret. I am a multiple submitter. I am guilty of sending the same story idea to more than one, uh—try eight—editors, all at the same time. There. I've said it. I feel like Ellen DeGeneres after her now-legendary prime time outing, relieved, but unsure of the ratings.

The term "multiple submitter" is spoken only in hushed tones by freelance writers, if acknowledged at all. And certainly never within ear shot of an editor—any editor, even an editor of the lowliest rag. But I am saying it, baring my soul to you. I promised you in the beginning of this book to tell you not only everything I've learned about writing women's stories but— equally important if you want to get your words read—everything I've learned about selling women's stories. And multiple submissions is the key.

You wonder if I felt a twinge of guilt sending the same idea to four, six, even eight editors all at once. Did my Catholic upbringing— being under the tutelage of nuns through high school and college— make me cringe as I committed this egregious act against the editorial world, you ask. Did I feel an upsurge of conscience as I personalized the editor's names and publications on the top of the letter, dropping in a few individual comments here and there? Did I hide behind Jackie-esque glasses as I dropped off the slew of the suspiciously similar-weight letters at the post office?

Not a chance.

My pulse raced. My blood tingled. It was an orgasmic high. All those ideas, all that potential for publication making its way from the Annapolis postmaster to Baltimore, then straight to Manhattan. Here, in action, was my strategy for conquering mountains of editorial madness.

Let me set the scene. Editors of large publications receive hundreds, sometimes thousands, of unsolicited submissions for story ideas, even complete articles, every month. Editors insist they weed through these queries as expediently as possible, and I believe them. But with staff meetings to attend, stories to assign, copy to edit and a publication to put out, hunting for a gem in what's typically a pile of trash is not top on their "to-do" list. One editor unabashedly admits to using this slush pile, as it's called, for extra seating during editorial meetings. So when you submit the one in a million appropriate submission, your letter is still relegated to the back of the line, to wait and wait and wait until the first reader, a newly minted Ivy League humanities graduate, gets around to it. Then you'd better hope it's not too close to quitting time. Truth is, it's easier to tuck that rejection slip in your self-addressed stamped envelope than work your suggestion up the ladder of editorial approval.

Assuming his date (yes, there are men on the editorial staffs of women's magazines) went well last night, this newbie first-reader directs your letter to a second pile—admittedly shorter, but still a pile—for perhaps a senior editor or a features editor to review. Days, maybe even weeks or months, pass before this happens. And if your idea makes this tighter cut, it's likely that it still has to be approved by the editor-in-chief, maybe even a whole editorial board, at their next meeting.

Here you are in Kansas City working up a sweat positive imaging and you haven't heard as much as a burp from anyone outside of the farm belt.

Truth is there'd be no problem and no justification for multiple submission if a positive portrait were developing deep within the editorial havens. You're a reasonable adult; you'd be patient. But odds are that what's happening is nothing. Even if months have gone by, chances are there's still a rejection slip with your name on it somewhere in your future. Problem is, by the time you learn the truth, that no news had not meant good news, your idea is no longer fresh and frisky and the blush of enthusiasm that kept you up half the night writing the query has withered. Even worse, you're convinced the editors are right, the idea stinks.

According to Leonard S. Bernstein, author of *Getting Published: The Writer in the Survival Zone*, on average, a good idea will sell on the 12th submission. Thus, with the one-publication-at-a-time system, you'd better be the rare, rare writer who is so oozing with confidence that, the day you finally receive rejection number 11, you tweak your query and resubmit to publication number 12. At this rate, it will take nearly two years for your query to find a home, assuming all your editors are conscientious about replying. Add another six months to a year for it to see print and a quarter of a decade's passed before idea meets ink.

The scenario's not much better at small publications because many have no assigned staff to handle the deluge of freelance ideas. An even darker reality is that a few, fortunately very few, editors of magazines of all sizes never respond at all to queries. Most won't admit this outright, but it seems to be happening more often.

So what's a writer to do? For one thing, don't take to heart editors' plea that "it's unfair to us if we spend all this time considering an idea and then find it's been taken by a competitor." It's also unfair for you to research and write a proposal, only to have it languish for months in an editorial office. Also, don't back down when they threaten never to work with you again if they catch you in such a despicable act. (Do you really believe any editor would reject a great idea simply to hold a grudge?) Remain stoic even when they insinuate you'll be blackballed among this very cozy pod of editors. Public relations types will tell you that getting your name out there, even if it's for negative reasons, is usually better than being ignored.

Instead of playing it their way, join us rules-busters. Forge ahead and multiple submit. For once, make the odds work for *you*. Consider this: more Americans are killed each year on highways than died in the Vietnam War. Knowing this, do you keep your car in the garage? Of course not. Chances are you'll never be seriously injured in a car accident, and chances are you'll never be caught multiple submitting. And the good news is, you will be published.

Still undecided? Consider the tale of two writers, my good friend Kathy and me. Twelve years ago we both began freelancing women's stories to magazines. I had a journalism degree and a newspaper background, but Kathy had a freer writing style, good ideas and loads of contacts, so I'd say we were evenly matched. Kathy succumbed to terminal freelance frustration years back, never relishing the satisfaction of being published beyond her hometown. As I may have mentioned earlier, my stories have appeared in the top women's magazines, as well as the far-reaching *Reader's Digest* and *The Saturday Evening Post*. Am I a better writer? More talented? More creative? I wish. The fact is, I'm more determined, more persistent and I am a confirmed multiple submitter. Kathy was not.

Let me tell you about my $50 experiment. Ten years ago I discovered that if I invest $50 in postage, and mail about a dozen large manila envelopes, each containing two or three query letters and copies of three or four published articles, in return I get a four-figure assignment. That's at least a thousand dollars, and more often two, three or four thousand on a $50 investment. Did my experiment ever fail? Twice. But that's in 12 active years. Give it a chance. (Considering inflation, invest $65, and please let me know what happens.)

Need more convincing? Consider how unlikely it is that two publications will want your idea, no matter how compelling. Let me explain. I'd consider a story published first in *Family Circle*, then reprinted as a *Reader's Digest* feature, to be a marketable idea. Still, I had sent that original query to nearly every woman's magazine and only *Family Circle* wanted it. True, this was earlier in my writing life, which brings us to the next point.

When you're first beginning to freelance you must cast a wide net. Just picture 1,500 unsolicited letters. This is the number a *Woman's*

> ❦ *I suppose you've already guessed my dirty little secret. I am a multiple submitter. I am guilty of sending the same story idea to more than one, huh—try eight—editors all at the same time.*

Day editor tells me she receives in one month. Starting out, try to shift the odds, just slightly, in your favor. Then as you develop relationships with editors, modify your marketing strategies. For instance, I have editors now who report back to me within a week or so saying whether they'll pass along the idea to their senior editors. Fair enough. I appreciate their attention and give them exclusive submissions because of it.

But this has taken years to develop, and I'll bet it would never have happened if I had not multiple submitted. For those editors with whom I've worked, but who do not treat me gently, I multiple submit. At the end of the query I note "concurrently submitted." But I don't say this until the last sentence because it's better to seduce them first with a great idea, then let them rush to be the first to assign it. And, yes, when I'm approaching editors I've never worked with before, I multiple submit—without comment.

Not all editors believe multiple submissions are wrong. Some realize that committed writers need to pay a mortgage, send kids to college and occasionally eat. We're not dilettantes shooting off an idea between croquet matches. We need to be published. Imagine any other salesperson giving a prospective client endless time to hold, inspect and monopolize a product. Editors respect writers who survive in one of the most competitive fields in the country. They depend on us and our ideas, and we won't be able to serve them if we're not making sales.

You're probably wondering if I've ever gotten caught multiple submitting? Yes, two times.

What happened? The first time, when an editor learned an idea had been sold elsewhere, she was repentant. She'd taken seven months, that's right—seven whole months—to respond. The second time, I groveled. This editor phoned within days of getting the query, and yes, she was angry that the story had already been taken by another magazine, and yes, she threatened to tell her assistants not to put my queries on the top of her pile. And yes, I felt guilty. Very guilty. I apologized, but not until I pleaded my case, then promised not to do it again—and I won't (see paragraph above about not multiple submitting to editors with whom you have a relationship). I even sent flowers. She wrote that she was leaving the magazine and invited me to submit ideas to her new publication.

The point is, multiple submissions get you and your work noticed. Once your ideas are being considered, back off from being the marketer extraordinaire—but just a little.

Hear Ye! Hear Ye!

MOST WRITERS ARE NOT VERY GOOD PROMOTERS of their work or themselves. We find the notion of marketing distasteful. It smacks of insincerity. The very term conjures up images of carnival hucksters, telephone solicitors or our neighbor who only phones when she's hosting one of those house parties where, embarrassed, we buy stuff we don't even like.

But the truth is, our writing is going to be read only by family, friends and unsuspecting colleagues who ask, "What are you working on now?" if we don't do at least a little bit of self-promotion.

I was asked to speak at a writers' conference in Washington D.C. When I picked up my name tag reading, "Freelance Writing Promotion Expert," I cringed. I wondered how anyone could have considered me such a thing. But the more I thought about it, I realized the coordinator was a former student of mine who once marveled at how I broke through freelance barriers. She knew something beyond divine providence had to account for it, and that something was promotion.

I struggled long and hard—well, actually it was less than an hour the night before the conference—wondering what I could offer. What had I done? What had others done to successfully promote their work? And more important, to promote themselves? Was there a magic bullet?

The more I thought about it, the clearer the answers became. The strategies had less to do with specifics and more to do with attitude. But I knew if I launched my lecture with this insight, the audience would head straight across the hall to hear the prominent New York agent. And, after all, there must be some tangible things one can do.

After grappling with how to rein in esoteric concepts, this is what I've come up with.

Believe in your product

Let's be up front, for most of us promotion stinks. It's easier to plan your funeral than to tell the world and its publishers, however subtly, that your writing deserves to be published. Thus we have to believe, from the bottom of our bellies, that we're fulfilling a need. That readers would be deprived, if only a smidgen, by not experiencing our point of view, our sensibilities on some speck of the universe.

That said, let's consider promoting our ideas first, then ourselves.

Looking back over my so-called breakthrough articles, those pieces that launched a relationship with a particular magazine editor, I detected a trend. Most of the article ideas fell into three categories: One, the true-life dramas that could only be obtained through me. It was a package deal. If they wanted the story they had to work with me.

Two, grunt work, blue-collar-work type stories whose ideas required me to melt into the phone, researching, making one last call, then another. For example, I did a story on premarriage classes for engaged couples. Feeling I had to know what was out there, I canvassed the country—by phone of course—surveying dozens of programs, ranging from Bible studies to courses that included Twister-style games.

And three, outright great pieces such as the exclusive story about Grace Corrigan, Christa McAuliffe's mother, on the 10-year anniversary of the Challenger explosion.

Notice none of these indulged my desire to wander off to Pilgrim's Creek and record in detail the death of a moth who flew into a candle flame. Nor did any of these stories fall into the category of generic ideas, those general interest topics that everyone, including staff writers and the hottest freelancers, competes to write.

These were strong ideas that promoted themselves. Make sure your ideas are just as strong, and they will help you with their promotion.

I once participated in a seminar given by lifestyle counselor Barbara Sher. Barbara is a study in savvy promotion. This therapist turned international lecturer and bestselling author has transformed conventional wisdom, like the power of believing in yourself and networking into a worldwide gig. Hundreds of other therapists—younger, sexier, smoother—boast better resumes than this self-described grandmother fairy godmother. So how does she do it? And how can we too?

Benefits.

Nothing new here, just a marketing principle worth repeating. Barbara always speaks benefits, not features. She begins at the end, inducing her listener to imagine her dreams coming true. Then she takes her back and walks her through the steps to create these benefits. You should do the same when you're pitching an idea.

Remember the query for my *Family Circle* article "Don't Pay For It—Trade For It!" began:

> If you've never wished upon a star, now's your
> chance. A diamond necklace, a romantic cruise, piano
> lessons, even cosmetic surgery can be yours without
> spending a dime—when you barter instead of buy.

I tempted the editor with benefits that could be realized by the reader of my piece. I didn't start off with statistics or an explanation of how to get these benefits, that came later.

OK. Now it's time to sell yourself. Just as you developed the idea, you now must develop a persona; become a personality to the editor. The same creativity that you put into your story idea you now put into creating a self-portrait. You must convince the editor that you are as compelling as your suggestion. But how? Consider these three points: credibility, politeness and self-confidence.

Credibility

Imagine an editor receiving your letter. He's never met you and, in fact, until the very moment that your query crossed his desk, he never knew you were alive. Now you're asking him to entrust his professional reputation to you. To most editors this is a far more nail-biting proposition than risking the payment of a small kill fee. Editors are judged by the company they keep, their stable of writers. And for junior editors you could theoretically make or break their career because the more stories they successfully shepherd into print, the quicker their names rise to the top of the publication's masthead, that front-of-the-publication list dictating editorial pecking order.

Think about it and you can understand their queasiness. How many of us have suffered when someone we trusted went strange on us, maybe a confidante who suddenly turns distant as a stranger in Grand Central Station? Editors worry about this. Can they depend on you to stick with the story through endless rewrites? Will your story hold up under the scrutiny of fact-checking? What if your life-partner splits or your child becomes ill—will you honor your commitment? Or will you use the miles that separate you as an escape from your responsibility?

Deadline. There's a reason the first part of this compound word is dead. There's little worse to an editor in a far-off city with a hole in his publication than hearing the endless ring of a freelancer's phone.

Farfetched?

According to an editor at one major publication, more than half of the freelancers given assignments fail to deliver. It was hard for me to fathom this, but he shook it off as fear of failure. Getting an assignment is as close to nirvana as writers get. The next high is seeing the story in print. But there are a lot of banana peels between assignment day and publication. Some writers are like the contestants on "Let's Make A Deal" who keep the color TV instead of trying for the Toyota Camry behind door number one, two or three. They can't bring themselves to chance the possibility that the editor will reject the story, so they never get around to submitting it.

What can *you* do to convince editors of your credibility? Begin with simple letterhead stationery that includes your fax and e-mail information. Keep it clean, and I don't mean just free of coffee stains—an editor at a bridal magazine once received a bloodstained query on what to do when your marriage sours.

Capitalize on your success. When you've been published, be sure to include the clip in your package. And when you make copies of the article, duplicate the cover of the publication too. If it's a publication the editor knows, you'll be piggybacking on the cachet of the magazine or newspaper. Their reputation becomes yours.

Earlier I mentioned multiple submissions and the value of creating a package of three autonomous queries all sent to the same editor in the same large manila envelope. Except for my students and myself, I don't know of anyone else who does this. (Until now!) It creates a positive impression because you stand out as a writer who's ambitious, creative and in it for the distance. In other words, a credible writer.

Politeness

Be sure every time you answer the phone—and I do mean every time—that you're polite and proper. I once accused a magazine's new editor of being a telephone solicitor and nearly hung up on her. Not a good idea.

Saying "Mary Jones" in lieu of a simple "hello" sounds extra professional—if you *are* Mary Jones, of course.

Avoid carrying on three-party conversations with editors and screaming kids, editors and barking dogs or editors and hungry husbands. This stuff counts.

How promptly you return phone calls also matters. A woman I know lost a successful working relationship with a Maryland regional magazine without being told exactly why. But those of us who know her think it might have had something to do with her being hard to reach. She returned calls late and periodically seemed to vanish. She lived by her schedule, allowing family problems to trip up her work. Friends hang on, publishers don't.

Same for fulfilling editor's requests. Commenting on the freelance dilemma from his side of the desk, one editor told me that when he asks one of his staff writers to give him more information on a piece, it's in by the end of the day. Ask the same from a freelancer and he hears a litany of reasons it's going to take at least a week: her mother-in-law's due and the house has just been attacked by giant black ants; or she's in the midst of a legal battle against her ex-husband for custody of their six kids—all under 8; or she's doubling up on therapy and will try writing in a prone position, but no promises.

Self-confidence

Let's turn to the intrinsic side of ourselves and consider how confidence factors into your image. Let me explain. After living in our house for 13 years, I finally took down the white sheer draperies covering our living and dining room windows and hired a decorator to sew Williamsburg style swags. But before commissioning this one decorator, I auditioned two others for their ideas.

The first woman took unconvincing, yet painstaking, effort to identify the exact shade of yellow on the walls and the precise rust color of the wing chairs. After all of this, she timidly offered me a sketch of blah white draperies trimmed with a yellow and rust braiding so slight I swear it would have been detectable only under a microscope. This isn't necessarily a bad thing if you hang out with researchers with holstered microscopes, but looking over last year's guest list of our hundred closest friends, I can't say one fits that description.

Decorator number two confessed that she wasn't sure what she'd do to trim the dining room's French door, although she'd surely adorn the other windows with material so rich it would slump into folds and puddle to the floor. Listening to her made me feel like I'd just finished an all-you-can-eat buffet. My stomach even bulged. But when she said, "If you don't like the French door bare, when we get everything up we could *try* to figure out then what to do with it." I grabbed my checkbook. We weren't going to *try* anything with my decorating budget.

Compare these weasel attitudes with the woman who got the job. As she looked at the bare windows, her eyes lit up, and she smiled a far away smile, as if she were falling in love or being released from an awful migraine. She envisioned the rooms transformed with the new draperies.

"They'll be elegant, but warm," she cooed as she embraced the window frames. "Can you see it?"

"Oh, yes. Oh, yes. Yes, I can," I enthused, sounding like Meg Ryan in the you-know-which scene of *When Harry Met Sally.* "Oooooooohhh, aaaaaah..." we harmonized like alley cats. And when our duet ended, I wasn't sure what I was *seeing*, but I was certain that my home was in good hands.

Promotion builds. You send a query and then you wait and wait and wait. Eventually you forget it and get on to the next idea. Some-

---

❦ *Some writers claim that publication is not what it's cracked up to be. The joy is in the writing they say. Don't believe them. They're fibbing.*

---

times something wonderful results from that query. Often a rejection arrives, or worse, depending on how you look at it, nothing happens at all. But if you transform yourself into an idea machine, churning out proposals, something good will happen. I promise.

One day an editor phones assigning you a story idea you submitted months earlier. You can barely recall what it was about, but the fee she's offering is several thousand dollars, so you manage to sound intelligent, then rush to your computer to resurrect the story.

Or an editor from a major magazine calls asking you to write for them after reading your story in a newspaper lining her mother's kitchen junk drawer.

Or after teaching local writing courses for pin money and friendship, you take your show on the road, as Ryan would say, and earn more in a day than you did in an entire month. Dreaming?

Not so. All three things have happened to me. And even better, things like this have happened to thousands of other writers. Your turn is next.

Editors want you to be happy when they give you an assignment, but they don't want you to be hungry. Restrain yourself from leaping into the phone with gratitude when they call with work. This sends an unsettling message.

Can you negotiate better terms in a contract? You can try, and editors will not get angry with you for asking—especially if you have written for them before. Besides fee and deadline, you'll want to be clear on what rights you are selling. Always try to relinquish only first North American serial rights. Some editors ask for all rights, a definite last resort for any freelance writer, and many editors are now requesting electronic rights. You should be paid extra for additional rights. (To learn more about this emerging debate between writers and editors contact the American Society of Journalists and Authors in New York City at 212-997-0947 or on the web: asja@compuserve.com— http:\\www. asja.org.)

🐦 🐦 🐦

Some writers claim that publication is not what it's cracked up to be. The joy is in the writing they say. Don't believe them. They're fibbing. If they really believe this then why do they work so hard to keep publishing? Why don't they just write and leave the publishing to us writers who love to share our words with readers?

There's a creative high in seeing a glimmer of an idea develop into a full feature story. Promoting yourself as a freelance writer of women's stories is a sport. If you thrill to the chase, you'll be happy every day you write a word, mail a query, check your telephone answering machine. This high is the real reward for getting the word out there that you're a good writer with a point of view to share with others.

It Happens

FOR ME, HALF THE JOY OF BEING A WRITER is teaching writing. When I'm not holed up in my study doing it, I'm traipsing across the United States and Canada talking about it in lectures, seminars and workshops. One particular program tells editors, writers and public relations types, from corporations, medical centers, colleges, government, the military and, of course, freelance writers, more than they ever want to know about feature writing, in eight hours.

The day is a blend of personal anecdotes, successes and sorrows, exercises stolen from here and there, the best of two writing degrees, hundreds of writing books and nearly 20 years of professional writing experience. I inject megadoses of encouragement into overworked, underappreciated professionals. Oh, we also do lunch. And, no, no one as yet has dared to say lunch is the best part—anyway not to my face at 5 p.m., when I could turn threatening.

Besides needing to please a savvy group of professionals, I also feel the pressure to answer to a kindly, Santa-type supervisor , Tom Hunter, himself a writer, editor and seminar presenter. I exhaust myself to earn great evaluations and pass them along to Tom. I even hand him the occasional bad ones. Like the one I received a few years back from a woman from a rural Maryland hospital who lambasted me because she couldn't concentrate waiting for dessert—we always hold brownies for a mid-afternoon sugar-surge.

It's amazing how thoughts of this nasty variety linger longer than the hundreds of fawning friendly ones—like the woman who declared that she'd like to put me in her pocket and take me home with her. Funny, I do remember that one. Anyway, Tom pays well and handles all marketing, hotel arrangements, even travel schedules. All I have to do is be perky, professional and show up. Sounds easy? It's not. Once, in particular, it wasn't easy at all.

Halfway through my spring seminars one year, I committed the worst faux pas in my entire professional life. But, being an optimist, I probed it for what it could add to my life—and yours.

Here's what happened.

The Monday and Tuesday of the week from hell I presented seminars in Tampa, Florida and Charlotte, North Carolina. Back home on Wednesday, I phoned hotels checking to be sure handouts for the next week's seminars had arrived and, later that day, mailed other packets. I also spoke with Tom's assistant about last minute sign-ups. All was cool, or so I thought. In my appointment book I had written, "Friday, April 10, Baltimore seminar."

Wednesday night, Allen, Ryan and I went out for pizza and later I talked on the phone with a friend. I planned to drive the 30 miles to Baltimore the next night, set up the seminar room and unwind, so I'd be ready for the first participant at 8 a.m. on Friday.

Thursday, April 10, I woke at 8:30 sharp. I hadn't set an alarm. By the time I walked downstairs to the kitchen to put on the coffee, I was experiencing a sickening sensation. *Could there be a seminar today?* There was no logical reason for me to think that. I grabbed the brochure and read, "Baltimore, April 10." I opened my appointment book: Thursday, April 10. I phoned the hotel pleading, "Today is not April 10th, is it?"

"Yes, it is," the voice on the other end replied, nonplussed.

At that moment I prayed something would swallow me. I looked at the clock on the stove. It was now 8:40 a.m. Thirty students were waiting in a hotel conference room 40 minutes away. The seminar officially began 10 minutes ago, although many of them had probably been milling about for nearly an hour. I phoned the hotel again, asking the clerk to please send someone into the seminar room immediately, apologize to the group for my being late and to promise them that I'd be there at 9:30.

I knew I was in no condition to drive to Baltimore and hunt for the hotel. I was panicked. I thought of all the things that were not done. The room was not set up with books and handouts. The flip chart was not ready. My notes were in shambles from the last seminar, and I didn't even have time for a shower. I phoned for a cab, splashed water on my face, threw on a dress, put four giant electric rollers in my hair and grabbed my makeup bag.

Inside the cab, I put on lipstick and mascara and tried to make sense of the jumble of papers that were to be the day's notes.

The driver was kind and understanding. If he thought I was a lunatic, he didn't say so. He studiously searched for the Hilton and when the numbers on the buildings suddenly began rising instead of falling he used his radio to summon a police escort to the hotel. With flip chart in hand and an old brown corduroy jacket thrown over a sleek black Jones of New York dress, I ran to the first bellman, begging him to direct me to the seminar room. He pointed and I ran to the second floor, breathless.

There 30 people sat, elbow-to-elbow, staring straight ahead as they had for more than an hour. It was now 9:45 a.m. I told myself again and again that this is not life threatening, but for a seminar leader it's a real downer. The group had a legitimate squawk. Would they tear me apart?

Still, I was relieved to at last be there. I groveled, I gushed, I told them the absolute, cross-my-heart-hope-to-die truth. I showed them the date written clearly in my appointment book: "Friday, April 10." I told them I copied it incorrectly from a schedule months before. I explained how I do everything to avoid anything like this ever happening. I looked them in the eye. They weren't hissing or even whispering. They were listening. They seemed to understand. I told them how very sorry I was, but that now we should begin. I had wasted enough of their very valuable time.

I took a deep breath, secured the flip chart over the stand and began speaking. I have no idea whether it was the aid of divine intervention, but amazingly the words flowed. I didn't glance at my notes and yet the ideas came. There were no big words or lofty thoughts, just anecdotes, little stories that illustrated principles that worked and didn't work for me and others through the years. Standing there with oily hair, little makeup and not even a watch, I was stripped naked of my professional armor. There was no pretense. I was simply a person who had screwed up royally.

As I paused to ask a question or glance at the flip chart, a stabbing thought kept recurring: *Did I realize what had just happened? And what would have happened if this seminar were in a far off city, like most are. What if I hadn't realized at all that there was a seminar today?* Each time this happened I felt like I was about to lose it, like I was having an out of body experience. Then I'd talk myself down. "Just keep going, one word at a time," I'd say.

When we broke for lunch, a woman from the front row came up and hugged me. "You were shaking when you came in," she said. She told me she felt the group understood, although none of them had awakened to 30 people waiting in another city.

I asked her what else I might do, and she suggested I tell them what they had missed.

When they returned from lunch, I explained that because of the time lost, we wouldn't be doing the writing assignment, but I would give them the exercise and they could stay past five and do it or send it to me.

During the break I thought hard about what I could offer them to make amends. I encouraged them to send me a feature article, even their whole publication if they had one, for my critique.

The afternoon went well, with lots of participation. At the end of the seminar I cringed as I passed out the evaluation forms. But when I read the comments later, I was surprised and heartened. Only one person mentioned wishing that we "could have begun on time." (I couldn't agree more.) But even his evaluation was positive. Later I received thank you letters from several members of the "Baltimore 30," as they named themselves. Of course, the letters included articles to be critiqued. Secretly I hoped that not all 30 participants would take me up on my offer. Still, I felt grateful for their understanding, and a little amazed.

I wondered what I could take away from this ordeal, besides being sure to double and triple check all seminar dates. (Allen's offered to stick them on his calendar too. And a friend has suggested a computer program that flashes reminders on the screen.) What principles were at work that made a potentially dreadful situation salvageable? And was there any connection between this gut-level communication with the group and the way we speak to our readers? I believe so.

Here are three commandments about writing that I learned from the Baltimore seminar.

Take action

As soon as I realized that morning that I had screwed up I swung into action, phoning the hotel, calling a cab, etc. I acknowledged my emotions, but didn't ponder them, didn't let them control me. I acted. Same with writing. Analysis is fine, but then get going. The mere act of putting one word after another, in spitfire succession, overcomes the critic, the censor, the little voice that tells you you're a fraud and you should be selling Amway.

Be real

Because I was so distraught, I didn't even consider concocting a bull story. A friend said I should have told the group my car broke down, then the cab was broadsided and on and on. I don't think so. The sheer momentum of my emotions, raw and on the surface, spoke volumes more than any fiction. My honest voice rang true. I did not possess the presence of mind to carry off a scam, but even the most successful con story would have paled in comparison to my true-life drama. As bizarre as it may have seemed to these professionals that I could have done such a thing, no one doubted my sincerity. After all, who would make up such a dumb story?

Ditto with writing. There is nothing as powerful as clean, honest, generic, no-bull writing. Readers can detect the fraud, the pretense, the veneer, the extra layer of gloss. It's so rare for someone to bare his soul, to show his warts, that it's the mightiest tool we have.

Do a little more

As with writing, effort is everything. I apologized but then went a step further. As the French would say, I gave them *lagniappe*, the something extra, the thirteenth doughnut to a dozen. The very next day, still emotionally wiped out, I wrote 30 letters, thanking each one for coming, saying I was sorry again for the mistake, and encouraged them to take me up on my critique offer.

So it is with writing. Make one more phone call after the one you thought was the last, ask the embarrassing, off-putting question you know your reader wants answered, do that one painful extra bit of research that brings a smile to your reader's lips or a tear to her eye.

Focus

MY FRIEND CAROLYN is one of the most creative, versatile people I've ever known. Carolyn lives nearby, but we
didn't become friends until she signed up for my writing class in Annapolis several years ago.

Writing was just one more interest Carolyn wanted to add to her
collection of ever-growing time suckers. She says she wants to create
jewelry from castoffs, play the violin again, read more, watch old movies a second and third time and host a 60s party with food from scratch.
So why not start writing?

In the beginning Carolyn was a model writing student, full of enthusiasm and story ideas. By class three Carolyn was engrossed in researching telephone scams targeting the elderly, while the rest of the
class was still waffling between queries about their mother messing up
their lives and how to lay a brick walk in a weekend. Carolyn's research
was first rate, top experts, hot stuff. And this was a full year before the
national media caught on to the story.

Are you wondering how you missed reading Carolyn's coup? Something happened between the time she put down the phone from her
last interview and before she began to write. What happened is that
Carolyn got another great idea—how safe is your water—and another
and still another. So rather than focus on the scam story and write a
proposal for this investigative piece, she began calling about researching second, third and fourth ideas.

"I just had to find out about pet-assisted therapy," she says.

"But I thought you were writing about safe drinking water?"

"Oh sure, I'm doing that too, after telephone scams."

But before any idea made it onto paper, she spun off into a fifth
and sixth project. Before long, Carolyn was tempted to get back into
jewelry making, "just for this week." But after her ad promoting her
gourmet fudge ran in *The Washington Post*, her plans to write faded like
the blooms on my over-watered African Violets.

Now all this would be fine if Carolyn were happy and confident and all those life-affirming adjectives that puff us up. But Carolyn is miserable. Her body can't keep up with her brain. And after bouncing from one project to another, she feels like she's ridden a pogo stick.

When I got to know Carolyn better, I learned this was chronic with her. The shame is that she could write some great stories—she could do a myriad of things well—if she could ever finish one. If she could ever focus.

By contrast our son, Brad, the medical student, was always the kind of kid who could study while the house fell apart around him. His powers of concentration are so strong that nothing, absolutely nothing, distracts him. I pity his wife someday when *she* wants some attention.

If you asked him his secret he'd probably look at you lamely and say just glue your rump to your chair. It may not be all that simple, but it's a start.

So you're thinking "Well that's too bad, but I'd never be like Carolyn." Hold on. Writing women's stories can turn you into a Carolyn. It's seductive; it sneaks up on you. The more you learn about it, the more you want to learn, and your frame of reference grows larger and larger. In the name of research, you stroll into Barnes and Noble. First, it's the writing section, then you mosey on over to women's studies, self-help, psychology. Soon it's new nonfiction, biography. Eventually you wake to the horrific realization that everything's relevant when you're writing about women.

Same with ideas. First you can't imagine what you'll write about. But after that first byline, you notice another possibility. And once your creativity begins flowing, you'll see ideas everywhere. Lynn, another writing friend, says there are days her idea scanner runs on overdrive. Stopped at a traffic light she spies a pedestrian who reminds her of a baby-sitter who was charged with child abuse and she mentally writes the lead to an essay. While waiting in line at the grocery store she piggybacks ideas off the coverlines of the magazines displayed at the register. Each day, when her hometown paper arrives, she sees national angles in the tiny town's news. Worse yet, some nights she can't fall asleep. Instead of sheep, she's counting bylines. This can make the rest of us who stare at a blank screen crazy with envy. But creativity left unchecked can be as worthless as a blank screen.

Let me explain. Remember the two kinds of thinkers we talked about earlier, holistic and linear? Holistic thinkers, usually thought to be women, see the whole story, then the details. They detect patterns, see relationships, join seemingly unrelated facts. Linear thinkers, thought more often to be men, build a story, piece-by-piece, then check to be sure it's solid. They also meet deadlines, no small feat.

Combining both types of thinking helps you to write incredibly creative stories—on time.

Getting bombarded with ideas? You've got two choices. You can become overwhelmed and not write anything, which is what happens to most of us, or you can prioritize. Yes, that's it. The same stuff you learned back in grade school. Label ideas A, B, C, according to how much they compel you to race to your computer and start writing. Write the A ones now. Save the B ones for later. And trash the Cs.

"Finish what you start" sounds so terribly 1950s, right up there with "eat everything on your plate," a command now bordering on child abuse. Yet there's nothing like "putting a piece to bed" as they used to say in the old newspaper days. It's a kick. Something you'll never know until your first story is done.

Truth

SOMETIMES SPECIAL ISSUES ARISE IN WRITING that can't be neatly labeled and filed into chapters. Instead they're so personal, so sticky, that you're not really sure what to do with them but you know you must address them.

Let's take the subject of truth. We all know that as writers we don't lie. We tell the truth. But on occasion the truth gets a bit muddled and right and wrong isn't always clear.

Let me give you an example. When I wrote about the mother and sister who had spent a lifetime searching for one another, I ended the drama with their emotional reunion and the promise that their lives would be forever intertwined. Well wouldn't you know it, before the story went to press, the newly found daughter and her mother were not speaking, and both women swore they never wanted to see one another again, not ever. So what's real here? Both were joyously reunited when I wrote the story. Is it my concern that life moved along and by the time the story was in the hands of readers it was as accurate as last week's *TV Guide*?

While researching the *Reader's Digest* drama about the toddler who was lost in the desert, the editor asked me if the mother and rescuer had ever spoken before beginning the search. "Could there be a moment when the mother pleads to the volunteer, 'You've got to find my baby. We can't let him die!'"

"Maybe," I said, "I'll find out."

Since then several editors have "outlined" moments or scenes they imagine might have occurred in stories, asking me to see if I can get something close to that. Lately I find myself imagining story scenes before they ask—and before I interview. Does that mean I'm thinking like an editor? Is this good? Is it clever or is it calculating? I'm just not sure.

Is it possible that by power of suggestion we're creating stories that *we* want—rather than what really happened? Are we tampering with the truth? Are eager-to-please subjects—and, yes, some subjects will say almost anything to see their stories in print—going along with what we imagine happening in these stories?

I suspect this imagining is one more leap in intuitive, sophisticated interviewing, if you want to call it that. And I can't say that it's all bad. It may, indeed, help a subject to focus, to recall a particularly pivotal point or an emotional moment. And most important, it may help us come home with a story that offers the reader a take-away feeling or message that is, after all, the whole point of a feature article.

But I also worry that there's some pretty sensitive stuff going on here just below the surface. In a perfect writing world with a perfect interviewer who ever so sensitively suggests such moments to a subject without a hint of anticipation or persuasion, this may be a wonderful technique. But in a less ideal situation, we may compromise the most important part of the stories we write: the truth.

One time a *Digest* editor was considering a story idea about an extraordinary mother, when she learned that this woman was in the throes of separating from her third husband. This fact caused the editor to dismiss the story, although the story itself had nothing to do with the woman's wifely skills, but spoke rather of her extraordinary gift as a mother. Still the editor believed her jaded marital past compromised her credibility as a heroine. "Why do we have to mention it?" I wondered aloud. The editor seemed shocked, explaining that honesty demanded full disclosure to the reader. Even if it wasn't particularly relevant? I wondered silently.

Yet this same magazine created a very clever play with words in the toddler rescue story. Take a look at this paragraph:

> **Then an astonishing thing happened. As if propelled by an unseen force, Kallie raised her nose into the air and began to track furiously. She led the women to the base of the mountain more than three miles from the camp, where they heard a faint cry—and another.**

Casually reading that last sentence which says that the dog led the women to the base of the mountain *more than three miles from the camp,* do you get the impression that the dog led the women three whole miles in one swoop of a miraculous scent? Most readers do. The truth is that the dog actually directed the women only a 150 feet or so in that last track. True, they were three miles from camp, but that was over the course of a four-day search. This reality makes the climax far less dramatic. I had written the story with the shorter distance, but in the edited version I noticed the clever switch in the reader's vantage point. Now are we wrong as writers if we write the truth, letter for letter, but the reader is misled, perhaps intentionally?

And what part do our personal feelings play when thinking about the truth? Let me explain what I mean. Most of the time when I write women's stories I am awestruck by these women who, even under the scrutiny of a writer's eye, remain bigger than life. They wrestle life's injustices into extraordinary feats. So it's a shock when occasionally the woman turns out to be just like us, replete with frailties. We're spoiled by their grander sisters and, although these plain Janes are true to their stories, they offer nothing more, such as inspiration. We're disappointed, and we wonder if it shows in our words.

Seldom, but it happens, you meet a woman who wants to write the story for you. At first you're grateful when she slips you a note with names and numbers of others to interview or she suggests locations for photo shoots. But when she takes over the interview, regaling you with anecdotes and telling you the points they make, then filling your bag with self-serving newspaper clippings, background and all sorts of information that "you need for your story," you'll wish you could fade into the wallpaper. The more she puts herself into the story, the more you pull yourself out. You lose heart. You feel yourself slipping away, her voice becoming distant.

She may be pushy, and even obnoxious, but is she violating any truth? Is what she's doing *really* so different from what we do when we orchestrate an interview and later write the story? Or are we just smoother? Or perhaps we're excused because we're writers? These are hard questions with no easy answers.

Intimacy

WHEN WE WRITE STORIES ABOUT WOMEN, we ask our subjects questions that we wouldn't ask our closest friends, and sometimes we broach this privacy membrane in a matter of hours or minutes of meeting them.

Because these women have stories to tell that interest us, stories we want to write, our attention is totally focused on them. Before the interview we've thought of what we're going to say, what questions we need answered. We're the perfect, knowledgeable conversationalist. Seldom has a woman had such attention. It's easy to understand how she can be charmed by us.

Occasionally we create such a comfortable faux social situation that the subject reveals things she's never told another soul. One mother confided that she had lost an infant to crib death and her other children—now all teens and within ear shot of our voices—never knew this. At that moment I wasn't sure I should know either. But once I had the information I felt in the awkward position of having to switch postures from one of a confidante to that of a journalist—whose first concern is not to the woman being interviewed but to the woman who will be reading the story. Could I convince her to let me write about it? Would I be morally wrong to try?

When your subject shares intimate aspects of herself with you, you have to wonder what, if any, obligation you have towards her when the story is finished. Here she's bared her soul to you. You've smiled, you've nodded attentively and you might have even acted as if you were her friend, and at that moment, you might have really believed you were. So now what? Can all that concern come to a close with the last question, or when your story's accepted or when it is published for all to read? When do you feel OK closing the door on your relationship?

I once heard that when Tom Clancy went to the Coast Guard headquarters in Washington D.C. to get background for one of his early novels, he wasted not a minute. He asked questions, got answers and was gone. Not a lot of time for civility. When I heard this, I thought his actions sounded brusque, but lately I wonder if he were acting more honestly than I.

What it comes down to is this: Do we owe our subjects anything more than a thank you?

Writers disagree on the answers, and I suspect that sometimes we, too, may vacillate in our thoughts. It gets confusing because we've been taught to leave our emotions out of a story. We have been trained to view things with objectivity. How can we justify turning a pure and perfectly professional meeting into a personal relationship? And yet, at times, how can we resist?

Sandy Barnes, the mother whose two young sons died tragically, is one woman whom I could not forget when I packed up my notebook. Her story touched me profoundly, and the weekend we spent together grew into a relationship of caring that continues today.

There have been others with whom I've promised, as I put down my pen, to keep in touch. The promise was made not out of obligation but out of expectation and yet I haven't. Although I think I was sincere when I said it, other stories and life filled in and apparently these women, many of whom, unlike Sandy Barnes, had spouses to share concerns, just didn't tug as strongly at my heartstrings.

Maybe the most we can hope to accomplish when we interview and write about women is what Pulitzer Prize winning writer Rick Bragg describes as "uncovering the dignity, the feeling that is already there."

Save the World

A NEW NOVELIST ADDRESSED our Hopkins writing seminar one day. She said she had spent nearly 10 years getting her book published and speculated that it might take another 10 to get anyone to read it. A second author declared that there are more people writing poetry today than reading poetry. He then added that even the poets don't want to read poetry, unless it's their own. What a thought.

It does make you wonder if the world really needs another writer. Will anyone be deprived if we never write another word? Sure the arts are important, but are we ever going to live long enough to read all the wonderful literature already written?

Will we wake one morning, realize we're 80 years old and say, "Gee, I'm glad I spent my life trying to get published?" Or will we have second thoughts about the difference we might have made if we chose to spend our time another way? Maybe we could have helped a child learn to read, cheered up a nursing home resident, counseled an abused wife, even walked an orphan dog at a shelter.

The thought distressed me, until I realized that as writers we can do all of the above and more. Instead of supporting the frail with our arms, we support them with our words. When we write about things that really matter, our struggles to write and publish make sense. We're no longer battling just for bylines.

Women's stories are by nature emotionally driven so it's a given that the issues we write about touch lives in ways we can only imagine. You'll never know how many people will live because you wrote about organ transplants, or how many relationships are mended when you tell stories of forgiveness. And service pieces, such as the ubiquitous how-to, help readers live fuller, happier lives.

Writing about causes close to your heart transforms an act of self-absorption into expression of concern for others. Our work changes lives one word at a time and this makes writing women's stories truly noble. Now go, and be wonderful. I'll see you in print.

About the Author

Donna Elizabeth Boetig is a freelance writer specializing in women's stories. Her articles have appeared in major publications, including *Reader's Digest, McCall's, Woman's Day, Family Circle,* and *The Saturday Evening Post.* She is a contributor to several books on writing. A former newspaper reporter, she earned her graduate degree in writing from The Johns Hopkins University. She teaches writing workshops throughout the United States and Canada and is available to teach workshops based on the principles in this book. She and her husband Allen are the parents of three sons. They share their Crownsville, Maryland home with two dogs and two cats.

To order an additional copy of this book
please call toll free (800) 497-4909.